FIN KENNEDY

Fin Kennedy is an award-w...
regularly produced in the U... ...He also teaches,
blogs, campaigns, fundraises and dramaturgs other writers –
with a particular focus on young people's projects in London's
East End. Since November 2013, Fin has been Artistic Director
of touring theatre company Tamasha.

Fin is a graduate of the MA Writing for Performance
programme at Goldsmiths College, London. Fin's first play
Protection was produced at Soho Theatre in 2003, where he was
also Pearson writer-in-residence.

His second play *How To Disappear Completely and Never Be
Found* won the 38th Arts Council John Whiting Award, and was
produced at Sheffield Crucible in 2007. It has since been
produced in London, America and Australia and become a firm
favourite with student and amateur performance groups. It is
among Nick Hern Books' most licensed plays.

Fin's first two plays for teenagers, *Locked In* and *We Are
Shadows* were produced by Half Moon Young People's Theatre
in 2006 and 2008 and toured nationally, the first in a long track
record of writing for young people.

Since 2007 Fin has been writer-in-residence at Mulberry School
for Girls in Tower Hamlets, where he co-founded Mulberry
Theatre Company, for whom he has written seven plays.
Mehndi Night (2007), *Stolen Secrets* (2008), and *The
Unravelling* (2009) all premiered at the Edinburgh Festival
Fringe, while *The Urban Girl's Guide to Camping* premiered at
Southwark Playhouse in 2010. All are published by Nick Hern
Books in *The Urban Girl's Guide to Camping and other plays*.

Fin's fifth play for Mulberry School, and the first in this volume,
The Dream Collector, was the inaugural production in Mulberry's
new onsite theatre in October 2013, while the sixth, *The Domino
Effect*, premiered at the 2014 Edinburgh Festival Fringe.

Mulberry Theatre Company made history in 2009 when they were awarded a Scotsman Fringe First for *The Unravelling*, the first time a British state school has ever received one.

Fin also writes for radio and has had three Afternoon Plays broadcast on BBC Radio 4 including *The Good Listener*, a returning series set inside Government Communications Headquarters (GCHQ).

As well as writing plays, Fin also has many years of experience teaching playwriting. Whilst Associate Artist at Tamasha he founded *Schoolwrights*, the UK's first playwrights-in-schools training scheme. As Artistic Director, he has launched Tamasha Playwrights, a new agency of playwrights-for-hire, offering diverse role models for young people's projects in inner-city schools.

Fin writes a widely-read theatre industry blog at www.finkennedy.blogspot.co.uk, is an occasional contributor to the *Guardian* and *The Stage* and a visiting tutor on the MA Dramatic Writing at Central Saint Martins.

Fin Kennedy

THE DOMINO EFFECT

and other plays for teenagers

The Dream Collector

Fast

The Domino Effect

NICK HERN BOOKS

London

www.nickhernbooks.co.uk

A Nick Hern Book

The Domino Effect and other plays for teenagers first published in Great Britain in 2015 as a paperback original by Nick Hern Books Limited, The Glasshouse, 49a Goldhawk Road, London W12 8QP

The Dream Collector copyright © 2015 Fin Kennedy
Fast copyright © 2015 Fin Kennedy
The Domino Effect copyright © 2015 Fin Kennedy

Fin Kennedy has asserted his moral right to be identified as the author of these works

Cover image: photo courtesy of Vicky Matthers and Words&Pictures

Designed and typeset by Nick Hern Books, London
Printed and bound in Great Britain by Mimeo Ltd, Huntingdon, Cambridgeshire PE29 6XX

A CIP catalogue record for this book is available from the British Library

ISBN 978 1 84842 468 5

Woodland
CARBON
www.woodlandcarbon.co.uk
NICK HERN BOOKS
Printed on Carbon Captured paper

Contents

Introduction
Fin Kennedy

I first experimented with writing for an ensemble in my very
first play for teenagers, *East End Tales*, a series of dramatic
poems about inner-city life, written for multiple voices and
inspired by articles in East London newspapers. At the time
(2004) I was writer-on-attachment at Half Moon Young
People's Theatre, developing my first professional play for
young audiences for a national tour. That play, *Locked In*,
involved only three actors, largely because they were all
professionals who needed paying – and also because the entire
show had to fit into the back of a van. *East End Tales*, however,
was the result of a short residency in an East London school,
into which Half Moon sent me as part of my own professional
development as I learned to write for their target age group.

Writing a play for young people themselves to perform, as
opposed to professional actors performing for an audience of
young people, is a very different thing. For a start, in the
former, large casts are actively encouraged so that as many
people as possible can take part. This presents challenges as
well as opportunities. Maintaining coherent storylines and
meaningful character arcs for ten, fifteen or even twenty named
roles is not always possible, especially when the overall running
time is unlikely to exceed forty-five minutes. Then there is the
nature of rehearsals stretching over weeks or even months, and
the likelihood of cast changes due to teenagers' busy lives,
clashes with other projects or just general dropouts.

One technique I developed to deal with these variables is a
choral writing style, which uses nameless narrators to introduce
and guide the telling of the story. This can accommodate
anything from two to twenty narrators in the chorus. Often the
language is in a playful, lyrical style, which makes the lines
easier to learn – the idea is that everyone learns the lot, so that
in the event of cast changes (or drying on stage) others can

cover the lines. This form also plays to one of teenagers' great strengths – acknowledging the audience and telling them a story directly. Young actors are naturally good at this, and audiences love its conspiratorial nature. Other, named parts can and do emerge, but the chorus of narrators is never far away.

The three plays contained in this volume are therefore for large casts of young actors aged thirteen to nineteen. Cast sizes can vary due to this ensemble style, but the minimum is about eight (for *The Domino Effect*, though it can be done with more), and the maximum about sixteen (for *The Dream Collector*). *Fast* is more fixed as it uses named characters throughout, and tries to do justice to giving each of them a journey, but even so it can be performed with either nine or twelve actors (depending on whether the four older parts double or are separated out). Ensemble casting can also include non-speaking parts, who can use physical theatre, dance and music to create stylised representations of the world of the play. In this respect, the only upper limit on cast size is the imagination of the company taking the play on.

Each script in this volume was developed with a different group of diverse young people in inner London, though the characters and stories are universal enough to suit most young people's groups. The specific circumstances of ethnicity, culture and geographical location are less important than a strong ensemble ethos. A willingness to experiment with a physical performance aesthetic will help significantly, as will a commitment to working together to create the onstage magic necessary to tell these stories in a way which will delight an audience, allow transitions to unfold smoothly, and communicate each story's emotional truth.

Each play was conceived under different circumstances and it may help those of you hoping to stage them if I tell you a little bit about how each of them came about.

The Dream Collector

The Dream Collector was the fifth play developed with my long-term collaborators, Mulberry School for Girls in Shadwell, East London, with whom I have been creating new plays for over ten years. (Our first four are also published by Nick Hern Books in *The Urban Girl's Guide to Camping and other plays*.) However, in 2012 we added a new twist. By this time our work had become known locally as a pioneering partnership between a playwright and an inner-city state school. In an effort to continually evolve the way we work together, and to share some of the expertise we had built up, we decided to reach out to another local school during the making of our next play, and see if it was possible to develop a new play across two schools simultaneously. I approached local comprehensive, St Paul's Way Trust School in Bow, who were eager to be involved.

The practicalities of such an arrangement at first appeared to be problematic. If I was the sole writer then clearly I could only be in one school at a time. Yet running joint sessions, in which one school's students would travel after school to attend workshops at their partner school, would soon become expensive and logistically difficult. With sessions having to start some time after 3.30 p.m. in order to allow the other school's students to arrive, what would the students already on site do in the meantime?

After some deliberation, our solution was simple. As the one who was the most easily mobile, why didn't I travel between schools, taking the ideas for the play with me? In this way we hit upon what turned out to be quite a neat model. After-school workshops were held twice a week on different days, one in each school. I would develop ideas with Mulberry in one session, then take them with me to St Paul's Way, presenting them to their students, developing them further, then taking the new ideas back with me to Mulberry the following week. The whole thing became like a long-distance version of the party game 'Consequences'. It was fun – each week the students were eager to see what new ideas the other school's group had added to their own. In this way, the two groups never actually met one another until the readthrough of the first draft of the complete play.

All this had an impact on the play's form. *The Dream Collector* concerns a Year-Eleven school group who go on a Media Studies trip to an isolated country house which had belonged to a black-and-white movie pioneer, Charles Somna. Upon arriving, they soon discover that Somna was responsible for much more than the creation of mere movies – as the inventor of the Somnagraph he had built the world's first machine for screening your dreams. Once they step through the movie screen and enter the Dreamworld, each of the young friends meets their dream double, the sinister Neverborn…

The idea of having essentially two casts within one play was deliberate. It was intended to allow two real casts to rehearse their parts separately if necessary. While the Neverborn are present during the journey to Charles Somna's house, the Real-World cast are not aware of them. Both casts could (in theory) rehearse their sections separately and come together later in the process to put the final show together. This could be useful in future iterations, if two groups within the same school cannot rehearse together for timetabling reasons.

However, once the play was written, it became clear that the logistics of joint rehearsals across two schools would be insurmountable. Who would direct the show? If it was to be two teachers, one in each school, how would creative responsibility be equitably shared? Would rehearsals have to wait each day for half the cast to show up from the other school? In which school would the set reside?

In the end, each school agreed to stage their own separate production. At first this seemed to be a pity, but the benefits soon became clear. Each school had co-commissioned the play via an equal financial investment, and that investment suddenly reached twice as many students. Eventually, each school's students were able to visit one another's production and discuss the creative choices made with a deep knowledge of the play. For some, this became a piece of coursework.

In terms of the education and theatre sectors working together in future, this got me thinking. If two or more schools co-commission a play from a writer, yet produce their own versions, suddenly the project becomes a lot more affordable.

It multiplies its reach, and the writer gets two (or more) productions all in one go. In this age of austerity, this kind of innovative thinking could well come into its own. If any schools reading this are interested in forming a consortium to work in this way to commission new work (and not just from me!) then I would be happy to advise – do get in touch.

Fast

Fast came out of a very different process altogether. It was commissioned by a theatre company rather than a school. Y Touring has for fifteen years been producing and touring plays for young people about complex, science-based issues. Their unique 'Theatre of Debate' format allows young audiences to be involved in the creation of new plays right from the start, by inviting them, along with the playwrights who will be creating the work, to workshop days in which scientific specialists present different perspectives on the issue under discussion. I was invited to attend the debate day surrounding diet, fast food and food security, which took place as part of the development of Sarah Daniels' 2014 play *Hungry*. My brief was to conceive an accompanying play for an ensemble of young actors along similar themes.

Fast concerns Cara, a sixteen-year-old student at a comprehensive in an unnamed small town, close to some countryside. Cara is from a farming family, and we learn that one year previously her father had committed suicide. When Cara's school holds a twenty-four-hour fast in aid of Oxfam, Cara decides she will not eat again until Tesco and the other suppliers, whom she holds responsible for driving her father to suicide, are held to account. The play touches on issues of diet, commerce, class, industrial farming, the environment, grief, austerity and friendship with (I hope) wit and a lightness of touch. In *Fast*, the ensemble are all named parts and as such have clear identities and character arcs, each with their own distinct view of Cara's actions. This allows for considerable ownership of each character by each cast member, and would lend the play to analysis and deconstruction, for example hot-seating each character to learn more about their background and views. *Fast* was workshopped at Regent High School in Camden before being performed by a young people's summer school cast in August 2014.

The Domino Effect

For *The Domino Effect* I returned once more to Mulberry School for Girls. In 2014, Mulberry was celebrating its fiftieth anniversary and was keen to take a new play to the Edinburgh Festival Fringe. Mulberry and I had built our reputations at Edinburgh, taking a play every year for three years between 2007 and 2009, with our third show, *The Unravelling*, scooping the *Scotsman*'s prestigious Fringe First Award. (All three of our Edinburgh plays, plus one other, are published in *The Urban Girl's Guide to Camping and other plays*).

The Domino Effect was conceived in summer 2013, while on a short break in France, during which I watched again one of my favourite films, Jean-Pierre Jeunet's *Amélie*. Hang on, I thought. This is a Mulberry story. Set in the inner city, with a teenage girl at its heart, *Amélie* is about a quiet deep-thinker with a rich imagination, which starts to spill out into the real world, until even she isn't sure what is and isn't real. I often met young women like this in Mulberry, though I often met loud extroverts too, but this seemed a good opportunity to develop a play looking at the interior worlds of these more introverted students (who are also not always the easiest students to engage in Drama). I started to wonder, what would an East London version of *Amélie* look like? As I knew Mulberry and its students so well, the school agreed for me to lead on writing a first draft then to workshop it with students afterwards.

Around the time I was sitting down to write the first draft, I was having some work done on my house. One morning, one of the builders came up to my study and handed me a set of dusty Victorian dominoes he had found underneath our floorboards. Playwrights can be superstitious about these sorts of signs arriving as some kind of heaven-sent inspiration, and I am no exception. The metaphor seemed to be perfect – dominoes, and the domino effect, as a cascading symbol of actions we set loose into the world, knowingly or not, from apparently insignificant beginnings. All the subsequent sessions at Mulberry confirmed that this idea captured the students' imaginations as much as it had captured mine. The resulting play about 'small actions, big effects, and mastering the law of unintended consequences' ended up securing us our first five-star Edinburgh review and a clutch of enthusiastic reviews comparing the dense, poetic text to Dylan Thomas's *Under Milk Wood*.

The Domino Effect was the first time Mulberry's Drama and Dance departments had collaborated on a show, and the script was conceived with this in mind. It is undoubtedly the most ambitious text I have ever written for a young people's group. The detail of the world it observes is not only about the audience seeing things through Amina's peculiarly observant eyes, it is about planting small references which will become significant later, and about charting the ripple of one's actions in an area of high-density living. In performance it requires crystal-clear diction, an ensemble that support each other instinctively, and the sharpest of physical-theatre aesthetics to bring to life the play's multiple locations in the blink of an eye. Every narrative section is intended to be physically animated onstage by the ensemble. The play will not work if everything stops for the narrative to be merely recited.

I have described *The Domino Effect* as a love letter to East London, and indeed to the wonderful Mulberry School, where I have spent a decade honing my craft. But I hope that the play will have a resonance far beyond the specific British-Bangladeshi community that inspired it. Ultimately, it is about showing young people that they have more power to change their own destinies than they could ever realise, whoever they are and wherever they are from. The play would suit mixed casts, though it also provides the opportunity for teachers to offer leading roles to Asian or Muslim students, and I would encourage them to do so.

Since writing these three plays I've been appointed Artistic Director of touring theatre company Tamasha, a new chapter for both me and the company. In the immediate future it means I'll be doing less writing of my own and more working with other writers to develop a new generation of dramatists. But I carry the inclusive, community-focused ethos which inspired these plays with me into my new role. Having an infrastructure opens up some exciting possibilities – such as Schoolwrights, Tamasha's pioneering new playwrights-in-schools training scheme, the first of its kind in the UK. If you are inspired by the plays in this volume I'd encourage you to get in touch with us to see how we might be able to work with your school, to support and develop the work your Drama department is doing. As a national touring company, Tamasha has national reach, so it is not necessary for your school to be in London or the south-east.

I could not finish an introduction to a collection of plays for young people in 2015, with a looming General Election, without some reference to the current Government's attempts to downgrade arts subjects, and especially Drama, in our nation's schools over the past five years. To be putting out a new volume of plays for schools at such a time feels positively defiant.

It is.

As I hope the plays in this volume show – and the many more by my colleagues still writing for young people, not to mention the Drama teachers up and down the country heroically defending their subject from a hostile Government – to teach Drama is to teach life. It is to teach how to be human, how to have agency, how to be heard. How to work through our differences, how to compromise, struggle, think and feel. How to be an intelligent, successful and humane society.

I've written elsewhere that teaching creativity in schools is like installing the software on which all the other information will run. Disincentivising it within the curriculum makes no sense. To teach Drama, creativity, the arts, is to teach how to think for oneself, and ultimately therefore, how to become oneself. What lesson could be more important than that?

I hope that this volume, in its own small way, will help keep our subject alive in the place where its flame can burn most brightly: in the next generation's hearts and minds.

April 2015

For more on Fin and his work, including how to get in touch, visit: www.finkennedy.co.uk

For more on Tamasha Theatre Company and its work visit: www.tamasha.org.uk

THE DREAM COLLECTOR

Author's Note

The play has been written for sixteen young actors aged fourteen to sixteen.

One group is a 'Real-World' twenty-first-century group of school students from East London. These eight all have names and individual identities.

The other is an ensemble cast of eight who inhabit the 'Dreamworld'. They are known as the Neverborn. Their world is like a black-and-white film, and is stylised and movement-based. They bring to life the other cast's dreams, and share lines as a chorus. Each Real-World cast member has a Neverborn who shadows them, and plays them in their dream sequence. This means there needs to be a minimum of eight Neverborn, but there could be more if a larger cast is available.

Note that the Real-World cast cannot see the Neverborn, except sometimes for the odd flicker. However they can, of course, see them when the Neverborn are on screen, and when they finally enter the Dreamworld.

The Neverborn are capable of silently manipulating the Real-World cast, a bit like puppeteers or hypnotists, sending them in certain directions at certain times, or prompting them to speak with a snap of their fingers. This can be played with in production, and is not always referred to in the script.

Note that the sections referred to as taking place 'on screen' do not necessarily have to be pre-recorded films. They could be realised more imaginatively, using live performance too.

The Dream Collector was first performed by Mulberry Theatre Company, as the inaugural production at the Mulberry and Bigland Green Centre, on 16 October 2013, with the following ensemble cast:

	'REAL-WORLD' CAST	NEVERBORN
RAPHAEL	Fatima Khatun	Afsana Yasmin
MADGE	Maria Amrin	Aisha Miah
NASIMA	Mina Begum	Basma Akouiz
JAYDEN	Muslima Sheikh	Rumana Miah
MACK	Nazia Salim	Syeda Thani
ALI	Promee Reza	
SURAYA	Sumaiyah Ahmed	
AMELIA	Wahida Tasnim	

Director   Shona Davidson
Set and Costume Designers   Barbara Fuchs,
                                                             Afsana Begum
Technical Director   Chris Stone

The play was developed across two schools simultaneously. A parallel premiere production was also performed at St Paul's Way Trust School on 4 December 2013, with the following ensemble cast:

	'REAL-WORLD' CAST	NEVERBORN
RAPHAEL	Jenna Islam	Julakha Begum
MADGE	Nabeela Hoque	Nazia Begum
NASIMA	Romaysa Azzoug	Abida Chowdhury
JAYDEN	Matthew Rano	Kamar El-Aslani
MACK	Ben Cribb	Muneem Hussain
ALI	Azhar Uddin	Alessanrdo Islam
SURAYA	Sherinne Ghoneim	Soraia Pinheiro
AMELIA	Beatrice Green	Saabira Tasneem
		Mahfuza Uddin

Creative Director and Producer	Kelly Jasor
Set/Costume Production	Liz Gaskell, Frances Beasley, Magdalena Plewa-Ould
Technical Lead/Lighting	Rob Yardley
Stage Manager	Stephenjohn Holgate
Assistant Stage Manager	Ming Liu
Music	Denzel Bunbury

Characters

REAL-WORLD CAST
All fourteen or fifteen-year-olds from a twenty-first-century
East London school:

MACK, *dreams about quantum mechanics*
AMELIA, *dreams about fashion*
MADGE, *dreams about animals*
ALI, *dreams about business*
JAYDEN, *dreams about ninjas*
SURAYA, *dreams about medicine*
RAPHAEL, *dreams about dying*
NASIMA, *dreams about the army*
TEACHER, *a part which can be pre-recorded and played as
    voice-over, or played by some of the students, or the
    Neverborn (or even a real teacher). This is a creative
    decision for the company.*

Ethnicity of these parts is not that important. It is also possible
for girls to play boys, if necessary.

THE NEVERBORN
Can be played by any young people with good physical-theatre
skills. They do not have individual character names and their
lines can be distributed among the group, as a chorus. Each new
line indicates a new speaker, though sometimes several can say
the same line. Play around with this. Sometimes they chant,
sometimes they sing – find their rhythm.

Gender and ethnicity of the Neverborn is not that important
either, though it would help if each had a passing similarity to
the Real-World character they shadow.

Together, this cast also play the imposing figure of CHARLES
SOMNA, an early black-and-white movie pioneer and inventor.
How this is achieved is a creative decision for each company.

Lights up. AMELIA, MACK, MADGE, ALI, JAYDEN, SURAYA, RAPHAEL *and* NASIMA *are onstage. They are asleep.*

The NEVERBORN *are also onstage, though they are invisible and inaudible to the* REAL-WORLD CAST (*mostly*).

Each of the sleeping characters has a school uniform laid out nearby, ready for the next day. As they speak, the NEVERBORN *remove the school uniform from* AMELIA*'s room and replace it with a green dress. One of the* NEVERBORN, *who shadows* AMELIA, *also wears a green dress.*

NEVERBORN. Sssssshhhhhh
      This is a story about dreams
      The vast eternal deep
      We enter when we sleep
      Ssssssshhhhhh.

   The REAL-WORLD CAST *all turn over together in their sleep.*

   This is a story about what it could mean
   To build a machine
   To view on a screen
   Our dreams
   Sssssssshhhhhh.

   The REAL-WORLD CAST *all turn back the other way in their sleep.*

   They start to stir
   The night abates
   Daylight yawns
   The world awakes.

   The NEVERBORN *withdraw to where they are less visible. The* REAL-WORLD CAST *each get out a smartphone or laptop.*

MADGE. Facebook: I'm awake. Who else is up? Share.

AMELIA. Me.

MACK. Me

ALI. Me.

SURAYA. Too early, man. Share.

MADGE. I had mad dreams. Share.

RAPHAEL. Yeah and me! Share.

ALI. I was riding on the back of a giant ant.

BOYS. Like!

SURAYA. I was sinking into a sofa made of chocolate.

GIRLS. Like!

MACK. I was killing aliens made of baked beans.

BOYS. Like!

RAPHAEL. I turned see-through, so everyone could see what I had for lunch.

ALL. Eurgh.

AMELIA. I was wearing a… (*Sees the dress laid out, frowns.*) green dress.

AMELIA *picks up the dress, shrugs and puts the dress on.*

NEVERBORN (*whisper*). Good girl.

JAYDEN. I don't even wanna talk about mine.

MADGE. I always think there's like this massive factory, all full of elves, and they've all got their little elf outfits on, and their little tools in their little hands and they're hammering away, building everyone's dreams, night after night.

NEVERBORN. If only she knew.

MADGE. Share.

NEVERBORN. She will.

GIRLS. Like.

BOYS. Weirdo.

NEVERBORN. Time to get them ready.

The NEVERBORN *snap their fingers and the* REAL-WORLD CAST *get ready for school, packing a bag, putting their school uniforms on, etc. (In reality they could be partially dressed already and just put on a school tie, headscarf or blazer, etc.)*

The NEVERBORN *take out clipboards and pencils. They make notes about each character as they discuss them, or read notes about them from their files.*

MADGE. School trip today!

ALL. Yay!

JAYDEN. Bor-ing.

AMELIA. Shut up, Jayden.

JAYDEN. What you all bringing?

AMELIA. Make-up.

GIRLS. Nice.

MACK. PSP.

BOYS. Cool.

MADGE. Tofu.

ALL. YUCK.

ALI. Sweets – to sell.

SURAYA. Crisps – to eat.

RAPHAEL. Medical wristband – just in case.

NASIMA. Army survival kit – just in case.

JAYDEN. It's some dusty old house, not World War Three.

ALI. What you bringing?

JAYDEN. Nothing

MACK. Not even a toothbrush?

JAYDEN. It's only one night.

RAPHAEL. Not even pants?

JAYDEN. These ones are good for at least another week.

MADGE. Boys are like animals.

BOYS. Woof.

SURAYA. I thought you liked animals.

MADGE. Only real ones.

The NEVERBORN *gather around* MADGE.

NEVERBORN. They call this one Madge
   We've been watching her
   From a family of butchers
   Or so our records say
   But also a vegetarian
   Hmm, interesting.

The NEVERBORN *note this down.*

MADGE. Animals feel pain, they have rights too.

NEVERBORN. It says here she works part time at London Zoo.

MADGE. That's because I want to be a vet.

AMELIA. But you're a butcher.

MADGE. No I'm not!

MACK. You sure you're not there undercover?

JAYDEN. Yeah, on behalf of the family.

RAPHAEL. Scoping the place out.

JAYDEN. Hustling some exotic meat for the family shop.

MADGE. Shut up, I would never do that!

MACK. Yeah, half a kilo of tiger steak please, Madge.

MADGE. I work in the insect enclosure *actually.*

NEVERBORN (*write*). In-sects
   Per-fect.

The REAL-WORLD CAST *have finished getting ready and
all meet up with their bags.*

BOYS. Alright.

GIRLS. Alright.

*They begin the walk to school together, immediately
separating into girls and boys. The following conversations
take place while they walk.*

JAYDEN. So what is this place today?

ALI. It's like a country house of some old geezer.

JAYDEN. Dusty, man.

RAPHAEL. Better than school.

MACK. There'll be a coach.

JAYDEN. I hate coaches.

ALI. You can show your arse to traffic out the back.

JAYDEN. I like coaches.

The NEVERBORN *gather around* MACK.

NEVERBORN. This one they call Mack.

ALI. Mack the Hack.

JAYDEN. King of the Nerds, what's up.

NEVERBORN. But this one has a trick up his sleeve.

MACK. Just seeing what the teachers are saying innit. Let's
    see…

    MACK *is fiddling with his PSP (Playstation Portable).*

NEVERBORN. The boy has somehow managed
    To access the main school server
    Using only his PSP
    PSP?
    Playstation Portable – try to keep up
    I'm a hundred years old
    That doesn't stop the rest of us.

MACK. Mr Campbell's asked Miss Singh out for a drink after
    work!

ALL. LET'S SEE!

They crowd round MACK*'s PSP.*

MADGE. We might have a school wedding!

JAYDEN. Eurgh I hope not.

School bells go.

TEACHER. Registration!

The class sit behind desks at registration.

MACK *and* MADGE *are next to each other.*

They smile at each other awkwardly.

MACK. Do you like quantum mechanics?

MADGE. I don't know what that means.

TEACHER. Amelia.

AMELIA. Here, miss.

MACK. It's like a branch of physics.

MADGE. Oh right.

TEACHER. Ali.

ALI. Here, miss.

MACK. It's amazing. It means there might be a Multiverse, that's like, loads of universes, all existing at the same time.

TEACHER. Suraya.

SURAYA. Here, miss.

MADGE. I dissected a frog in science yesterday. Doing it made me cry, but now I understand frogs so I can cure one if it gets sick. Does that make it worth it?

TEACHER. Raphael.

RAPHAEL. Here, miss.

MACK. Did you know some people think the Multiverse was created by giant lizards?

MADGE. A frog's an amphibian not a lizard.

TEACHER. Jayden.

JAYDEN. Miss, if a geek and a nerd had a baby, would the baby be a neek or a gerd?

TEACHER. Don't be silly.

JAYDEN. I'm not.

TEACHER. Are you here or aren't you?

JAYDEN. Not really.

TEACHER. Well, thank goodness for that.

NEVERBORN. This one they call Jayden
Neither a geek
Nor a nerd.

JAYDEN. No way, man.

NEVERBORN. But he does seem to think he's a ninja.

JAYDEN. I'm a blue belt in karate actually.

AMELIA. You're a black belt in getting on our nerves.

NEVERBORN. The Year-Ten bad boy
Troubled
Troubling
Why do we have no data on his family?
Perhaps they never existed
Not possible
It is for us.

RAPHAEL. I'd like to do karate. Does your dad take you?

JAYDEN. No.

MACK *and* ALI *gesture silently to* RAPHAEL *to shut up*.

RAPHAEL. Your mum then.

MACK *and* ALI *continue to gesture*.

JAYDEN. Is that any of your business?

RAPHAEL. Just wondering…

JAYDEN. Well, don't.

RAPHAEL.… if they could take me too.

JAYDEN. Would you shut up about my parents, man!

ALI. Allow it, Jay, he's new.

MACK. Yeah, he doesn't know.

   JAYDEN *stomps off*.

RAPHAEL. Know what?

MACK. Jayden's parents are… (*Draws his finger across his throat*.)

RAPHAEL. No way.

ALI. Yeah.

MACK. He lives with his cousins now.

RAPHAEL. That's awful. What happened?

ALI. Nobody knows.

MACK. Nobody wants to know.

RAPHAEL. I should say sorry.

AMELIA. Don't bother.

ALI. Yeah let him cool off.

AMELIA. He's such an idiot.

MACK/ALI. Amelia!

AMELIA. What? I know he's been through a lot but it's no excuse.

NEVERBORN. This one they call Amelia
   Clever
   But arrogant
   With a tendency to stand up to authority.

AMELIA. Miss, you've put a spelling mistake on the board.

NEVERBORN. Our files show she has access to funds
   Make-up

Clothes
Jewellery
MP3 players
We detect ambivalence among the others.

SURAYA. You look nice, Ames.

MADGE. Love the dress.

NASIMA. I didn't know it was non-uniform day.

AMELIA. It's not.

SURAYA. Won't they send you home?

AMELIA. It's a school trip. I've paid.

MADGE *and* NASIMA *make faces behind* AMELIA*'s back.*

SURAYA. Amelia, I got you a Dr Pepper.

AMELIA. Oh my favourite, wicked, thanks.

SURAYA *gives* AMELIA *a can of Dr Pepper.* AMELIA *opens it and drinks some.*

SURAYA. Can I have a sip?

AMELIA. No, sorry, I'm well thirsty.

NEVERBORN (*write*). Doctor… Pepper
Pepper doctor
Hmmm.

Some school bells go.

ALI *flips open a briefcase he has been holding. It is full of sweets, arranged in rows like merchandise for sale.*

ALI. Roll up, roll up! It's sugar time!

The others crowd round, some of them buy sweets (*it is important that at least* JAYDEN *does*).

Forget breakfast, lunch and dinner, sugar is energy and energy is sugar. Stock up now for the journey ahead. All the sweets and chocolate you could ever wish for, all the stuff that's banned in the school canteen, get it right here, the sweets of your dreams! What do I have for you today, ladies

and gents? I got Fruit Ninjas, I got Hubba Bubba, I got
Haribo Starmix, I got Jelly Bellies, Mars bars, M&Ms, come
and get it, first come first served!

NEVERBORN. They call this one Ali
Otherwise known as Ali Sugar.

ALI. Lord Sugar to you.

NEVERBORN. After some sort of businessman?
Another one that's lost on me.

RAPHAEL. How come you're cheaper than the shops?

ALI. What can I say? Welcome to Aladdin's cave.

NEVERBORN (*write*). Cost
(*Write*.) Value.

Some school bells go.

ALI. Alright, shop's shut, people, get out of here.

ALI *snaps his briefcase shut and everyone disperses except
for* NASIMA. *They both look a bit shifty.*

Alright.

NASIMA. Alright.

ALI. What you got for me then?

NASIMA *opens up a bag.* ALI *looks inside.*

NEVERBORN. They call this one Nasima
A dark soul
Conflicted
Pulled between opposites.

NASIMA (*to* ALI). Sherbert Fountains, Turkish Delight, Cherry
Drops, Fisherman's Friend.

ALI. Fisherman's Friend? They're rank.

NASIMA. My Auntie Zora just got 'em in, I don't even know
what they are.

ALI. Trust me, just try one. It'll make your face fall off.

NASIMA. Whatever.

ALI. I'll take everything except them.

NASIMA. Fine.

    ALI *takes out some money.*

ALI. Shouldn't be nicking off your auntie anyway.

NASIMA. It's never bothered you before.

ALI. I didn't know it was your auntie's shop.

NASIMA. Gotta save up for my wedding, haven't I.

ALI. Thought you was joining the army?

NASIMA. I am.

ALI. You're a girl.

NASIMA. Dad wanted a boy.

ALI. You need to make up your mind.

NASIMA. I can do both, it is the twenty-first century.

ALI. Yeah, but what's marriage about? Babies. Life. What's the
army about? Killing. Death.

NASIMA. Do you want this stuff or not?

ALI. Yeah, fiver for the lot.

NASIMA. Done.

NEVERBORN. She does not know who she is
Perhaps a shock will do the trick
(*They write.*) Shock.

    She hands him the bag and he hands her a fiver.

    NASIMA *goes.*

    JAYDEN *approaches* AMELIA. *He holds out a box of
sweets.*

AMELIA. What?

JAYDEN. Fruit Ninja.

AMELIA. No thanks.

JAYDEN. I got them for you.

AMELIA. You've opened them.

JAYDEN. We could share.

AMELIA. And why would I wanna do that?

JAYDEN. I dunno.

AMELIA. Stick 'em up your nose.

> JAYDEN *sticks one up his nose.*

> You are such a loser.

> SURAYA *approaches* ALI.

SURAYA. Hey, Ali, you got any prawn-cocktail crisps?

ALI. Nah I'm sold out, man.

SURAYA. I really need some.

NEVERBORN. This one is nocturnal
A sufferer of insomnia
Tricky
Perhaps studying medicine means she'll find a cure
Perhaps
They call her Suraya
Meaning star
Though her tastes lie in the ocean not the sky.

MACK. Do you survive entirely on prawn-cocktail crisps?

SURAYA. So what if I do?

AMELIA. That's not very healthy is it – doctor.

SURAYA. Shut up, all you drink is Dr Pepper.

ALI. Can't help you, sorry. Try tomorrow.

SURAYA. What am I gonna do till then?

NEVERBORN. What shall we do with her?
We must make her understand
(*Write.*) Drawn... to prawns.

ALI *goes*. RAPHAEL *comes up to* SURAYA, *he is out of breath and panicky. He clutches his chest.*

RAPHAEL. Suraya... I'm feeling... really... breathless... and I think... I might be...

SURAYA. Alright, alright, calm down

SURAYA *sits* RAPHAEL *down and tries to calm him.*

NEVERBORN. This one is known as Raphael
A newcomer
Records show he has a hole in the heart
He has lived all his life in the shadow of death
Useful.

SURAYA *takes out a stethoscope and listens to* RAPHAEL's *chest.*

RAPHAEL. Jayden... jumped out on me... and...

SURAYA. Sssh, you gotta relax, Raph, remember?

RAPHAEL. Am I dying?

SURAYA. No.

RAPHAEL. But the hole... in my heart... when I get a shock...

SURAYA. You're not dying.

RAPHAEL. Is that your medical opinion?

SURAYA (*hesitates*). Yes.

NEVERBORN. These two appear to be friends
Or is it something more?

The NEVERBORN *click their fingers and the lights dim. They click them again and some slow jam comes on.*

SURAYA. How you feeling now?

RAPHAEL. Scared.

SURAYA. Don't be.

RAPHAEL. I don't wanna die alone.

SURAYA. You won't. Not while I'm here.

RAPHAEL. Thanks, Suraya.

They sit together for a moment. SURAYA *puts her head on* RAPHAEL*'s shoulder. The* NEVERBORN *sprinkle something onto her and she closes her eyes. The music plays.*

NEVERBORN (*whisper*). Twins.

RAPHAEL. Suraya?

SURAYA *has gone to sleep.*

NEVERBORN (*whisper*). Three... two... one...

Suddenly the school bells go. SURAYA *and* RAPHAEL *jump up.*

The music stops and the lights go back to normal.

TEACHER. Alright, listen up, please, Year Ten. As you know you are all off timetable today –

ALL. YAY!

TEACHER. – but this is in order to go on the Media Studies field trip. I hope I need not remind you that this is *still work.*

ALL. BOO.

TEACHER. Your coach is waiting.

The NEVERBORN *take out a toy coach, the* REAL-WORLD CAST *gather round.*

[*Just a suggestion – you can create the coach however you want.*]

Right, are we all here?

ALL. YES, MISS.

TEACHER. Good. Now, a little background.

The coach sets off.

Somna House is over a hundred years old. It was built by Charles Somna, the famous early-movie pioneer.

JAYDEN. Never heard of him.

TEACHER. Well, I suggest you read up on him, Jayden, because worksheets about Somna and his black-and-white films will be handed out throughout the day.

JAYDEN. Black and white? Bor-ing.

SURAYA. Shut up, Jayden.

MADGE (*looking at phone*). Says here Charles Somna invented the Somnagraph, an early form of film camera.

JAYDEN. Oh stop, you're sending me to sleep.

AMELIA. Well, we're all really excited.

JAYDEN. Yeah but you're geeks.

MACK. Somnagraph… why does that sound weird? (*Fiddles with PSP.*)

TEACHER. Perhaps it will interest you to know that Somna's wife was a famous actress of her day.

JAYDEN. Was she fit?

ALL. SHUT UP, JAYDEN.

TEACHER. Cecilia Somna was tragically killed on a film set while shooting one of her husband's many movies.

JAYDEN. Cecilia? That's a stupid name.

AMELIA. Shut up, Jayden.

JAYDEN. Like yours.

AMELIA. My name's Amelia not Cecilia.

JAYDEN. Exactly.

ALI. How did she die?

TEACHER. An unsecured stage light fell on her head.

JAYDEN. Haha, that's funny.

NASIMA. What's funny about it?

JAYDEN. Just a little light bulb? What a wuss.

AMELIA. Durr, don't you know anything? Stage lights weigh a tonne.

TEACHER. It's true, she was killed instantly.

RAPHAEL. Ouch.

TEACHER. And pretty soon after that, Charles Somna himself mysteriously disappeared.

MACK. Whoa.

AMELIA. Really?

ALI. Is that cos he did it?

JAYDEN. Yeah, did he kill her?

MADGE. You mean it wasn't an accident?

TEACHER. Nobody knows.

SURAYA. I'm a bit creeped out by that.

NASIMA. Me too.

JAYDEN. Miss, what if *we* mysteriously disappear while we're there?

TEACHER. In your case, Jayden, quite a few of us would be rather relieved.

Everyone except RAPHAEL *laughs and points at* JAYDEN.

ALL. AH-HA, HAHAHA.

TEACHER. Settle down, you've got a long journey ahead!

MACK. She ain't kidding.

AMELIA. Miss, we've been driving for ages.

MADGE. Are we there yet?

ALI. Is this still London?

JAYDEN. It goes on forever.

SURAYA. Wait, there's a field.

RAPHAEL. And another!

NASIMA. Everything's turning green.

MACK. Like someone's chucked paint over the world.

The NEVERBORN *chuck green paint over the world.*

The coach weaves among it.

RAPHAEL. Look! A sheep.

NASIMA. I ain't never seen a sheep before.

MACK. I have.

AMELIA. TV don't count.

MACK. Then I haven't

MADGE. There's loads – ten, twenty.

ALI. Fifty maybe.

NEVERBORN. Count them.

SURAYA. One.

RAPHAEL. Two

NASIMA. Three.

MACK. Four.

They yawn and their counting slows down.

AMELIA. Fiiive.

MADGE. Siiix.

ALI. Seveeeeeeeen.

NEVERBORN. Sssshhhhhhheep
Ssssssleeeeeeep.

The REAL-WORLD CAST *fall asleep on the coach.*

The NEVERBORN *assemble a large country house around the sleeping cast. They click their fingers and the* REAL-WORLD CAST *wake up.*

RAPHAEL. Oh my God. Guys… Guys! Look at this mad house!

The others rub their eyes and look. The NEVERBORN *are still around, creating some of the effects of the house, but they don't say as much from now on.*

ALI. Whoa! This geezer had some serious dough, innit.

TEACHER. Everybody, off!

They get off, get their bags, and look around.

SURAYA. How long were we asleep?

RAPHAEL. Ages, look at the sky. Sun's setting.

SURAYA. Like the colour of prawn cocktail.

TEACHER. Where is everyone? They knew we were coming.
Stay here.
Don't wander off.

The REAL-WORLD CAST exchange glances.

ALL. LET'S WANDER OFF

The creak of a huge wooden door swinging open.

NASIMA. Oh my days!

JAYDEN. Check this place out!

MACK. My whole flat could fit in this hallway.

SURAYA. It's like Hogwarts!

RAPHAEL. Sssh!

NASIMA. You'll get us in trouble.

They tiptoe further in.

AMELIA. Check out the posters.

*The NEVERBORN create old movie-poster images as they
pass.*

MACK. Must be from the guy's old movies.

AMELIA. Charles Summer.

MADGE. Somna.

AMELIA. Whatever.

ALI. I wanna see some.

JAYDEN. I don't – boring.

SURAYA. Hang on. Are they posters?

RAPHAEL. Yeah, they look… lifelike.

NASIMA. Real.

They stop in front of one of the images, which depicts the NEVERBORN *in the green dress being struck on the head by a large stage light.*

MACK. Oh my God, that must be the guy's wife.

AMELIA. Yeah, getting… killed.

MADGE. That's horrible.

ALI. Yeah, why would that be here?

RAPHAEL. I'm scared.

SURAYA. Yeah, maybe we should wait outside.

NEVERBORN (*whisper*). Sssssstay.

The NEVERBORN *pluck feathers from a pillow, and scatter them in a trail along the floor.*

MACK. I'm tired.

AMELIA. Yeah, it's late.

MADGE. It's cold outside.

ALI. Let's keep going.

SURAYA. Yeah, let's stay.

The cast follow the feathers, almost as if they are sleepwalking.

NEVERBORN (*whisper*). This way
(*Whisper.*) Downstairs
(*Whisper.*) Deeper
(*Whisper.*) Sleeeeep.

The cast walk downstairs, led by the NEVERBORN.

MACK *takes out his PSP.*

MACK. Hang on a minute.

AMELIA. Yeah.

MADGE. This is.

ALI. Yeah.

SURAYA. Dark.

RAPHAEL. Scary.

NASIMA. Steep.

MACK. My PSP says we're going down.

JAYDEN. Down where?

MACK. Just down.

JAYDEN. So what? It's an adventure.

NEVERBORN (*whisper*). Yesssss.

AMELIA. But we don't know where it goes.

NEVERBORN (*whisper*). Cccccccinema.

AMELIA. What did you say?

SURAYA. I didn't say anything.

RAPHAEL. This sort of thing is really bad for my heart!

NEVERBORN (*whisper*). Welcome.

NASIMA. Wait, there's a door.

ALI. There's a sign.

ALL. 'WELCOME.'

MACK. I don't feel very welcome.

AMELIA. In fact.

MADGE. Yeah.

ALI. Maybe we should go back up.

JAYDEN. Don't be stupid.

SURAYA. Yeah.

NASIMA. I spose we've come this far.

JAYDEN. Don't you wanna see what's inside?

NEVERBORN (*whisper*). Inside.

They push the door open.

AMELIA. Oh my days.

SURAYA. A dusty.

RAPHAEL. Musty

NASIMA. Rusty.

MACK. Old.

ALL. CINEMA!

They rush inside.

AMELIA. Oh my God.

MADGE. Look at this place!

ALI. Old seats.

JAYDEN. Red velvet.

SURAYA. Brass lamps.

RAPHAEL. Beautiful.

MACK. Brass statues.

AMELIA. Crimson curtains.

MADGE. The smell of dust.

ALI. Fabric.

JAYDEN. Adventure.

NASIMA. And ancient popcorn.

They discover various objects in the room.

SURAYA. An old popcorn machine!

RAPHAEL. A wheely ice-cream box!

MACK. An old Wurlitzer organ!

NASIMA. And an old... whatever this thing is.

They all go over to look at what NASIMA *has found, except for* MACK, *who goes over to the Wurlitzer organ and fiddles with it.*

AMELIA. That – is an old-style movie projector.

MADGE. Wicked!

NASIMA. How do you know?

JAYDEN. Do you reckon they've got *Night at the Museum 2*?

AMELIA. Don't be stupid.

JAYDEN. I'm not.

ALI. It's old films, innit.

SURAYA. Like what the guy who built the house must've made.

JAYDEN. You mean like, black and white?

ALL. YEAH.

JAYDEN. That's rubbish, man.

AMELIA. No it's not.

MADGE. Let's watch one.

ALL. YEAH.

The Wurlitzer organ suddenly blasts out music.

MACK *leaps away from it.*

MACK. Whoa!

ALI. What you doing, man?

MACK. I just wanted to look at it!

AMELIA. Turn it down, you'll wake up the whole house!

MACK. I didn't touch it!

The music continues to play.

Suddenly the lights go out. They scream.

JAYDEN. Shut up, man!

MADGE. Who did that?

RAPHAEL. I'm scared.

MACK. Just stay still – something's going on.

The curtains at one end of the room whirr open automatically.

Behind them is a movie screen.

The projector whirrs into life, making them jump.
It projects an image onto the screen, a black-and-white
movie plate bearing the words: 'Insert Coin'.

AMELIA. Oh my God.

MADGE. Oh my God.

SURAYA. Oh my God.

ALI. It just came to life.

MACK. No it didn't.

NASIMA. It did.

MACK. Nothing just comes to life.

SURAYA. Ghosts do.

MACK. It's a machine. It's just doing what it's programmed to
do. Someone put a coin in.

MADGE. No way.

ALI. Uh-uh.

SURAYA. Not me.

AMELIA. I will.

JAYDEN. Nice one, Amelia.

AMELIA. I'm not scared.

AMELIA *puts a coin into the projector, which whirrs. The*
others settle down to watch. The screen flickers into life.
Some music plays.

A black-and-white cast fade into view. AMELIA *is played by*
her NEVERBORN *double, who also wears a green dress.*

ALI. Oh my God.

SURAYA. Amelia, is that you?

JAYDEN. Yo, what is she doing in the film?

RAPHAEL. Amelia?

JAYDEN. It's in black and white.

MACK. All except for her dress.

MADGE. Yeah it's like the one she's wearing.

ALI. That is too weird.

NASIMA. Ames?

JAYDEN. Is this some time-travel thing?

AMELIA. I don't know!

On screen, the black-and-white cast enact a scene.

NEVERBORN. Sit back
Relax
Breeeeathe.

The NEVERBORN start to sing softly.

There's a hole in your middle
Amelia
Amelia
There's a hole in your middle
Amelia
A hole.

The black-and-white AMELIA mimes screaming as she looks down at herself. There is a gaping hole in the centre of her chest.

Real AMELIA in the cinema is horrified.

AMELIA. Oh my God!

The NEVERBORN pull on white coats.

Onscreen AMELIA faints, they catch her, and lay her out on an operating table.

NEVERBORN. We can fix it
    We can heal it
    Don't hesitate to operate
    Exfoliate and medicate
    Cancel out the emptiness
    With sweepings
    Swill
    Slop.

AMELIA. WHO THE HELL ARE YOU?

NEVERBORN. We… are Dr Pepper.

On screen, the NEVERBORN *take out jars of pepper and sprinkle it onto* AMELIA*'s open wound. Then, they take out lots of litter – crisp packets, drinks cans, etc. – and cram it into the hole.*

    Fill it up
    Fill it up
    Fill it up with fluff

    Fill it up
    Fill it up
    Fill it up with stuff.

AMELIA. Stop it!
    Get off!
    Get off me!
    (*To the others.*) I can't watch this!

AMELIA *covers her eyes.*

Just as she does so, the screen flickers to darkness and the projector whirrs off.

The film and the cast disappear.

The 'Insert Coin' screen comes back on.

AMELIA *is upset. Some of the others go to her.*

MADGE. Are you alright?

AMELIA. What do you think!

SURAYA. Come here, babes.

ALI. What the hell was that?

NASIMA. That was like Amelia's own personal horror film.

MADGE. Just leave her alone.

NASIMA. Just saying.

AMELIA. I'm scared.

SURAYA. Me too.

AMELIA. I mean, what was that supposed to mean? Am I gonna die?

RAPHAEL. We're all gonna die, aren't we?

MADGE. Raph!

RAPHAEL. I mean, one day. I've got a hole as well, haven't I? It's scary. I can come to the hospital with you if you like. Get it checked out.

AMELIA *takes* RAPHAEL*'s hand.*

MACK. I don't think that's what it means.

SURAYA. Maybe we should get out of here.

MACK. I need to try something first.

MACK *takes out a coin and goes up to the projector.*

AMELIA. Wait.

MADGE. Don't.

SURAYA. Not again.

AMELIA. I couldn't take any more.

MACK. It won't be about you this time. I promise.

ALI. How do you know?

MACK. Just trust me, yeah.

MACK *inserts his coin.*

The lights dim, the music starts and the projector whirrs into life.

A figure like MACK *appears on screen.*

ALI. Is that you?

JAYDEN. That looks nothing like you.

MACK. Just watch – I think I know what's gonna happen.

NEVERBORN. Tock
    Tick
    Tock
    Tick
    Clocks go back
    Space-time snaps
    Clocks go back
    Space-time snaps.

MADGE. Space-time?

MACK. Yeah, it's like, reality.

MADGE. 'Reality snaps'?

MACK. It's something I worry about, when the clocks go back.

There is a huge ripping noise.

On screen, space-time snaps and an alternative dimension emerges.

NEVERBORN. Time
    Space
    Eternity
    No more future
    No more past
    Did we mention the alternative dimension?
    Did we mention the alternative dimension?

MACK. Oh, man, I remember this bit.

AMELIA. You've seen this before?

NEVERBORN. Logic dictates
    The lizards await
    Monsters in vermilion
    A trillion reptilians
    Creators of the Multiverse

Hear
Them
ROAR.

A trillion lizards roar.

Tongues like a meteorite
Red in tooth
Red in claw
Feel
Them
BITE.

On screen, the lizards prepare to bite.

MACK. No!

Suddenly the screen cuts out and the room returns to normal.

MACK *exhales.*

Whoa. That was intense.

AMELIA. That was just as scary as mine!

MACK. I didn't say it wouldn't be scary, did I?

JAYDEN. Lizards?

MACK. Yeah.

JAYDEN. What the hell?

ALI. Man, that is deep.

NASIMA. That made *no* sense.

SURAYA. So how does any of that help us work out what's
going on?

MACK. I'll tell you how: because that was a dream I
sometimes have.

MADGE. What?

NASIMA. These are old movies, Mack.

MACK. No. This – (*Points to the projector.*) is not a movie
projector. It's a Somnagraph.

MADGE. A what?

MACK. I've been thinking about it for ages, but I think I've worked it out.

RAPHAEL. Worked what out?

MACK. Somna means sleep.

SURAYA. Like insomnia!

MACK. Exactly. And graph means write.

AMELIA. Like photograph. To write with light.

MACK. Right. So this isn't a film projector. It's a machine for screening your dreams.

They all turn to look at the Somnagraph.

Pause.

Then:

ALI. I want a go!

SURAYA. My turn next!

NASIMA. I'm going next!

RAPHAEL. I got my coin ready!

MADGE. Get away from it!

They all scramble to get to the Somnagraph. MADGE *gets to it first and puts her coin in.*

ALI. Madge!

SURAYA. I wanted a go!

AMELIA. Are you mad? It's horrible.

MADGE. I wanna see for myself.

The lights darken, the organ plays, and the projector whirrs. On screen, a version of MADGE *fades into view. There is a buzzing, clicking noise.*

Oh my God. It's me.

MACK. What's all that buzzing?

NEVERBORN. Praying mantis
    Termites
    Ticks
    Legs go scuttle
    Jaws go click.

On screen, thousands of insects appear.

    Spiders
    Hornets
    Mites and fleas
    Aphids
    Bedbugs
    Beetles
    Bees.

The insects swarm over MADGE.

MADGE. This is horrible!

NEVERBORN. Swarming hordes and flying clouds
    Plagues of locusts overcrowd
    Hair and skin contamination
    Teeming thriving infestation.

MADGE. Get them off me!

NASIMA. It's like *I'm a Celebrity*!

MADGE. I don't care!

NEVERBORN. Let the amphibians feast!
    Ribbit!
    Let the amphibians feast!

On screen, a giant frog appears and licks all the insects off
MADGE.

MADGE. Slimy!

NEVERBORN. Death
    Death
    Death to the frog
    Death
    Death
    Death to the frog.

A giant insect appears and eats the frog.

Daddy longlegs has to die
Mummy frog won't let this lie.

An even bigger frog appears and eats the giant insect.

MADGE. Stop killing each other!!

The screen flickers off and 'Insert Coin' comes back on.

JAYDEN. That was stupid.

MACK. No it wasn't.

NASIMA. I think you need to give up the zoo job.

MADGE. Is that what it means?

NASIMA. Pfff, who the hell knows.

MACK. It's a dream, innit.

ALI. My turn!

ALI gets to the Somnagraph first and puts in his coin.

A version of himself appears on screen, sitting on a throne, tossing sweets to the crowd below.

NEVERBORN. Ali Sugar
Ali Sugar
Saccharine king
Caliph of confectionery
And every sweet thing
With a heart of stone
He rules his candy throne
Except
Except
In this province of plenty
Famine stalks the land.

Some NEVERBORN appear to be starving.

Sweets sweets
But nothing to eat
Sweets sweets
But nothing to eat.

A female NEVERBORN *approaches* ALI *on his throne.*

ALI. That's my mum. What's she doing there?

NEVERBORN. Ali, Ali, what have you done?
Ali, Ali, what have you done?

Another NEVERBORN *plays* ALI*'s brother.*

ALI. That's my little brother. They're starving, why are they starving?

NEVERBORN. Sweets sweets
But nothing to eat
Sweets sweets
But nothing to eat.

ALI. I thought I made us rich!

NEVERBORN. There's nothing inside
So they died
Nothing inside
So they died
(*Fades out.*) Nothing inside so they died.

The screen flickers off. Everyone sits in silence for a moment.

ALI *is trying not to cry.*

MACK. Mate…

JAYDEN. Yeah…

RAPHAEL. Are you –

ALI. I don't wanna talk about it.

MACK. But –

ALI. I DON'T. (*Pause.*) Alright?

MACK. Whatever you say, man. Whatever you say.

Pause.

AMELIA. This is getting kinda weird.

MADGE. Yeah.

AMELIA. I mean maybe we should, you know.

RAPHAEL. Yeah.

AMELIA. Get out of here.

SURAYA. I want a go.

MADGE. Really?

SURAYA. Yeah.

AMELIA. Why?

SURAYA. I have to know. Have to see.

MACK. But it doesn't mean anything.

SURAYA. It does! Look at Ali.

> ALI *is sitting in silence on his own.*

> His dream meant something to him, didn't it? Well, I wanna see mine.

> SURAYA *puts her coin in the Somnagraph.*

> *Underwater sounds begin.*

> *Some pink blobs fade into view.*

> Are those… prawns?

> *Music plays.*

> *On screen, the prawns do a synchronised dance.*

> *The dance is gentle and soothing.*

> *The dance ends.*

> *The prawns take a bow.*

> *The movie ends, the lights go up and the 'Insert Coin' screen comes back on.*

MACK. What, is that it?

JAYDEN. Yeah, that was rubbish, man.

MADGE. Oh, I liked it.

AMELIA. Me too.

MADGE. They did a little dance.

NASIMA. Yeah, it was funny.

ALI. You need to lay off them crisps, Suraya.

MACK. Too right, they're messing with your head.

SURAYA. But I wanna know what it means.

JAYDEN. Means you're crazy.

MADGE. No it don't.

RAPHAEL. I thought you said you'd know.

SURAYA. I thought I would too. But I don't. Why don't you
have a go?

RAPHAEL. I don't really want to.

NASIMA. I'll do it.

JAYDEN. This'll be good.

ALI. Yeah, no one knows what's going on in Nasima's head.

JAYDEN. No one wants to.

NASIMA. Shut up, mine's gonna be the best dream *ever.*

NASIMA *goes over to the Somnagraph and puts her coin in.*

The lights dim and NASIMA*'s dream begins.*

On screen, NASIMA *is relaxing on a tropical beach.*

NEVERBORN. Queen Nasima
On the beach
Sun and sand
Stress can't reach.

NASIMA. Niiiice. Told you.

ALI. Wait a sec. What's that?

NASIMA. Where?

ALI. Something's in the water.

NEVERBORN. Haha
Heehee
There's clowns in the sea

Haha
Heehee
There's clowns in the sea.

Clowns walk out of the sea and towards NASIMA.

NASIMA. I hate clowns!

NEVERBORN. Shoot them dead
Shoot them dead
Shoot them dead with a Fisherman's Friend.

On screen, NASIMA *takes out a gun and loads it up with
Fisherman's Friends. She fires at the clowns and they
crumple. Their clown masks fall off to reveal a woman's face
beneath each.*

But faces fall
Revealing Auntie Zora.

NASIMA. Oh my God.

NEVERBORN. Who's the clown now, Nasima?
Who's the clown now?

NASIMA. Auntie Zora! I'm sorry.

*As the clown masks hit the sand, they transform into
newborn babies.*

Their crying fills the air.

NEVERBORN. Faces fall
And babies start to call
Faces fall
And babies start to call.

NASIMA. What?

NEVERBORN. Babies on the beach
Too many to reach
Too many
Too many
Too many to reach.

*The movie ends, the lights go up and the 'Insert Coin' screen
comes back on.*

MACK. That was the weirdest one yet.

ALI. I know, innit.

MACK. I mean, clowns?

ALI. Yeah, and babies?

RAPHAEL. My heart's going like the clappers – that's not good.

JAYDEN. And why was your auntie in it?

ALI. I know why.

NASIMA. Yeah, shut up, Ali.

JAYDEN. It was like a computer game.

MACK. Not any game I've played.

JAYDEN. Except for I'd have shot all the babies as well.

AMELIA. Shut up, Jayden.

JAYDEN. They were making a horrible noise.

AMELIA. You're a horrible noise.

NASIMA (*to* JAYDEN). Why don't you go next then?

JAYDEN. Nah, man.

SURAYA. Yeah, you haven't been yet.

JAYDEN. Neither has Raphael.

ALI. Why not you?

JAYDEN. It's Raph's turn.

AMELIA. Well, I wanna see *your* dream.

ALI. Yeah.

JAYDEN. Well, I don't.

RAPHAEL. It's fine, I know what mine will be.

    RAPHAEL *goes to the machine and takes out his coin.*

SURAYA. You sure about this?

RAPHAEL. Yeah. It'll be the two boys.

SURAYA. Two boys?

RAPHAEL. Twins. In the forest.

RAPHAEL *puts his coin in and the movie starts.*

On screen, two boys appear, both look like RAPHAEL.

They are walking through a forest.

NEVERBORN. Ssssssh
Through the silent forest
The twins go slow
Where are they headed?
Nobody knows.

The twins reach the edge of a lake.

See them walking
To the edge of the lake
One keeps walking
The other just waits.

On screen, one of the boys walks into the lake, while the other waits on the bank.

He watches his brother
Go up to his waist
Up to his chest
And up to his face
Opens his mouth
But he can't make a sound
Just watches his brother
Sink down and down
Sink down and down.

The twin in the lake disappears from view.

The movie ends, the lights go up and the 'Insert Coin' screen comes back on.

MACK. How did you know it would be that?

RAPHAEL. Cos I dream it every night.

AMELIA. What does it mean?

RAPHAEL *shrugs*.

JAYDEN. We should get out of here.

MACK. Yeah, it'll be late.

AMELIA. Yeah, teachers might notice we've gone.

MADGE. Wait – Jayden hasn't been yet.

ALI. Oh yeah.

SURAYA. Have we all done it except you?

JAYDEN. I dunno.

NASIMA. Yeah we have.

AMELIA. Come on, ninja, we wanna see yours.

JAYDEN. Well, I don't.

MACK. Why not?

JAYDEN. I just don't.

AMELIA. We all did it.

ALI. Yeah, you scared or something?

JAYDEN. No.

SURAYA. What then?

JAYDEN. I don't wanna.

RAPHAEL. Look, if he doesn't want to, he doesn't have to.

NASIMA. It's cos he's scared.

JAYDEN. No it's not.

AMELIA. Jayden's scared!

ALI. Jayden's scared!

MACK. Jayden's scared!

JAYDEN. No I'm not!

AMELIA. Well, why not do it then?

NASIMA. Yeah, why not?

ALL (*chanting*). WHY NOT, WHY NOT, WHY NOT.

JAYDEN (*yells*). COS I KNOW WHAT IT'LL BE!

Pause.

ALI. Alright, man.

MACK. Sorry.

AMELIA. No need to shout.

JAYDEN. Just leave it, yeah.

MACK. Right.

ALI. Alright.

Pause.

MACK. Let's get out of here.

AMELIA. Yeah.

They get up.

JAYDEN. Whoa. Where's the door gone?

MADGE. Oh my God.

ALI. It was right there.

NEVERBORN (*whisper*). The screen.

AMELIA. Did you say something?

SURAYA. No.

RAPHAEL. Where the hell is the door?

NASIMA. Mack?

MACK. I dunno, let me think.

MACK consults his PSP.

The screen shimmers at one end of the room.

NEVERBORN (*whisper*). The screen.

AMELIA. There!

MADGE. Ssh!

ALI. Yeah, I definitely heard something then.

MADGE. SSH! Mack's thinking.

MACK. The PSP's pointing…

MADGE. Where?

MACK. Over there.

MACK *points to the screen.*

AMELIA. Oh, man.

RAPHAEL. Oh no – no way.

ALI. That's not out, Mack. That's in.

JAYDEN. What choice do we have?

AMELIA. Jayden's right. And who knows, maybe we'll even find out what our crazy dreams were all about.

NEVERBORN. Yeeessss.

They take each other's hands.

MACK. Then let's do this. Ready?

AMELIA/JAYDEN. Yeah.

MADGE. Not really.

SURAYA. No.

RAPHAEL. Ready as I'll ever be I spose.

AMELIA. One. Two. Three. Run!

ALI. Run?

AMELIA. Run!

ALL. RUN!
RUUUUUUUUN!!

They run through the screen [possibly in slow motion].

There is a blast of white noise, like static, and the cinema disappears.

They scream.

Wind rushes past them.

They land with a jolt.

AMELIA. Everyone okay?

MACK. Yeah.

MADGE. Think so.

ALI. Are we alive?

JAYDEN. What *is* this place?

They are in a black-and-white movie studio.

Everything is in black and white around them – including props, costumes and other objects from the dreams they watched earlier.

Perhaps there is a director's chair, clapperboard and old-fashioned camera.

The NEVERBORN *appear. The* REAL-WORLD CAST *can see them fully now.*

NEVERBORN. Welcome
Welcome
Welcome…
To our world.

MADGE. It's the cast! The black-and-white cast from the dreams!

NEVERBORN. You are us
And we are you
We know exactly what
You're going to do.

Each NEVERBORN *examines their double.*

JAYDEN. Crazy. Like looking in the mirror.

The black-and-white cast mirror the movements of the REAL-WORLD CAST *exactly.*

[*This could become a short movement sequence featuring all sixteen actors, as if the black-and-white cast are hypnotising the* REAL-WORLD CAST, *shaping and twisting them around like puppets.*]

AMELIA. Wait. They're hypnotising us. Snap out of it, everyone!

They snap out of it.

MACK (*to* NEVERBORN). What's going on?

NASIMA. Where are we?

AMELIA. Who are you lot?

MADGE. How come you know our dreams?

ALI. And how the hell do we get out of here?

NEVERBORN. Calm yourselves, young ones
    You are beyond dreaming
    This – is Somna City
    Where dreams are made.

The NEVERBORN *smile.*

AMELIA. Who are you then?

NEVERBORN. We are the Neverborn.

ALI. The what?

NEVERBORN. Once, we were just like you
    Young
    Curious
    Ignorant
    Foolish.

AMELIA. Speak for yourself.

NEVERBORN. A school group
    Invited by Charles Somna himself
    Into his house
    Into his cinema
    Into his world
    It was 1929.

SURAYA. No way.

RAPHAEL. You're school students?

NASIMA. From 1929? Get out. That means you'd be about, like, a hundred years old or something.

NEVERBORN. Yesssss
  But the Neverborn do not grow old.

AMELIA. Mack, please tell me you understand this.

MACK. I don't understand anything.

ALI. What does your PSP say?

MACK. It's blank. We're totally off the map.

NEVERBORN. Like you, we were tempted inside
  Like you, we stepped through the screen
  Like you, we disappeared.

ALI. Uh-oh.

  The NEVERBORN *click their fingers and an hourglass
  appears and starts counting down.*

NEVERBORN. In Somna City
  Memories of you fade
  You become un-missed
  Unknown
  Until all trace of you has gone
  As if you were never born
  Out there – already your families are waking up
  Getting ready
  Going about their day
  Not having noticed
  That you are missing
  Looooook.

  They see this on a screen somewhere, like CCTV.

  The hourglass continues to pour.

RAPHAEL. Oh my God.

MACK. That's my sister.

AMELIA. That's my brother.

MADGE. That's my mum.

NEVERBORN. When the sand runs out
  You will have disappeared completely

Photos – gone
Memories – erased
Facebook – deleted
School, friends, family – all forgotten.

The NEVERBORN *snap their fingers, and all around them, objects from the set start to disappear* [*just a suggestion – not an essential effect*].

You will have become Neverborn.
And we can finally rest.

ALL. WHAT?

NEVERBORN. Now please
Put these on
You have a lot to learn
And very little time
Before darkness falls once more
And your work must begin.

The NEVERBORN *hand each of the* REAL-WORLD CAST *a set of black-and-white clothes, indicating they should get changed.*

AMELIA *throws the black-and-white clothes to the floor.*

AMELIA. No way, forget it.

NEVERBORN (*in unison*). Pick up your uniform!

AMELIA. No! I wanna speak to Charles Somna.

MADGE. Amelia, careful!

AMELIA. I wanna speak to the Dream Collector himself!

NEVERBORN (*in unison*). But you already are.

AMELIA. What?

NEVERBORN (*in unison*). In here, everything becomes one.

The NEVERBORN *rise up and become* CHARLES SOMNA.

He towers over them. The REAL-WORLD CAST *are terrified and cower in a corner.*

Only AMELIA *stands her ground.*

SOMNA. WELL WELL WELL
  THE NEXT NEVERBORN.

AMELIA. No chance! We've got a bone to pick with you.

MADGE. Amelia – don't!

AMELIA. Relax, this is what I do. (*To* SOMNA.) You've
  trapped us here – that's kidnapping. And if you keep us here
  – that's murder.

SOMNA. IT IS ONLY MURDER IF YOU HAD LIVED.

AMELIA. We have lives to lead.

SOMNA. NOT ANY MORE.

MACK. Don't listen to him, I think he's one of those lizards!

SOMNA. I NEED THE YOUNG
  YOUR DREAMS POWER MY SEARCH
  COME
  BE NEVERBORN
  AND YOU SHALL NEVER DIE.

AMELIA. Hang on – your search for what?

SOMNA. FOR MY WIFE OF COURSE.

MADGE. Oh my God.

SOMNA. FOR MY BEAUTIFUL WIFE.

MADGE. His wife was the actress who died!

SOMNA. THEY SAY I KILLED HER – LIES!

MADGE. I never said that!

SOMNA. IT WAS A TRAGEDY!

AMELIA. Alright, calm down.

SOMNA. THE LIGHT FELL ON HER HEAD!

  SOMNA *swoops around the stage. Lights flash on and off.*

AMELIA. Alright, it was an accident! We know that.

SOMNA. SHE IS HERE SOMEWHERE
I WOULD SEE HER IN MY DREAMS.

MACK. So you built the Somnagraph. It all makes sense.

SOMNA. MY LIFE'S WORK
TO FIND HER AGAIN.

ALI. But you haven't

SOMNA. IT IS LIKE CHASING AN ECHO
I CATCH A GLIMPSE
BUT THEN SHE IS GONE.

SURAYA. Maybe it's time to stop looking.

SOMNA. NEVER!

RAPHAEL. Maybe memories are meant to fade. Maybe they're
designed that way for a reason.

AMELIA. Look, it's a sad story, Mr Somna. We're all really
sorry for you. But it's even sadder for those who got sucked
in after you. They had nothing to do with this.

SOMNA. MY DARLING WIFE.

SOMNA *begins to cry.*

AMELIA. The Somnagraph's dangerous. It's like a door that's
still open. You need to shut it down.

SOMNA. IN HER GREEN DRESS.

NASIMA. This is pointless. He's completely round the bend.

SOMNA. HER BEAUTIFUL... GREEN... DRESS.

SOMNA *notices* AMELIA *is wearing a green dress. So does
everyone else.*

ALI. Uh-oh.

MACK. Oh, man.

MADGE. Oh no.

SURAYA. That's a –

JAYDEN. Yeah.

ALL. GREEN DRESS.

SOMNA. CECILIA?

AMELIA. No – Amelia. My name's Amelia.

SOMNA. CECILIA!

AMELIA. There was another girl in a green dress.

SOMNA. MY DARLING.

AMELIA. She was right here! Where's she gone?

SOMNA. I HAVE FOUND YOU.

AMELIA. No! This whole thing was a set-up!

SOMNA *advances on* AMELIA.

JAYDEN. Get away from her.

JAYDEN *steps between* SOMNA *and* AMELIA. *He holds a large wooden samurai sword.*

SOMNA. STEP ASIDE, BOY.

JAYDEN. No.

SOMNA. SHE IS STAYING.

JAYDEN. She's coming with us.

ALI. Where did he get that sword from?

MACK. I don't know.

ALI. I want one.

SOMNA. LET HER STAY
AND THE REST OF YOU CAN GO.

JAYDEN. Take me.

SURAYA. What?

JAYDEN. Take me instead.

MADGE. Jayden!

SOMNA. YOU ARE NOT MY WIFE.

JAYDEN. Neither is she. The Neverborn tricked you. Tricked us all. Amelia's not the one you're looking for. Your search isn't over.

SOMNA. THEN I NEED YOU ALL.

JAYDEN. No, just me.

ALI. Jay, no.

MACK. *Think* about this, man.

JAYDEN. I'll be as good as ten of them.

SOMNA. WHY?

JAYDEN. I'll be the best Neverborn you ever had.

SOMNA. WHY?

JAYDEN. Because I know what it's like to lose someone! To spend every waking hour wanting them back.

SOMNA. WHO IS IT YOU SEEK?

JAYDEN. My parents. Maybe down here, I might actually find them.

A whisper echoes around the stage: 'Jaydeeeen'.

Mum? Dad? I can hear them. They're here somewhere, I know it. I want to stay.

ALI. Bruv… don't do this.

NASIMA. Yeah, we won't let you.

JAYDEN. But why should I go back? What have I got to go back for? I'd rather stay here, and be a dream.

MACK. The sand timer! Look!

MADGE. We have to get out of here.

ALI. How?

MACK. I don't know!

MACK frantically fiddles with his PSP.

SOMNA advances on AMELIA. JAYDEN raises his sword.

JAYDEN (*to* SOMNA). Any closer, and I'll give you a nightmare of your own. Understand?

AMELIA. He has to tell us how to get out.

SOMNA. THE LIGHT FELL ON HER HEAD... ON HER HEAD.

AMELIA. Yeah, we know. Look, Mr Somna, the sand's running out.

SOMNA. THE LIGHT... MY POOR, POOR WIFE.

AMELIA. Please!

MACK. Wait. He's telling us the answer.

ALI. What?

MADGE. How?

ALI. No he's not.

NASIMA. He's just blethering on.

SOMNA. MY FAULT, ALL MY FAULT.

NASIMA. See?

MACK. But think about it. This whole thing is a dream, right? And how do you wake up from a dream?

SOMNA. THE LIGHT.

MACK. With light.

SOMNA. ON HER HEAD.

MACK. By making *light* fall on your *head*... He's telling us the way out!

MADGE. Curtains – open the curtains!

MACK. Exactly!

They find some large curtains and prepare to pull them back.

AMELIA. Wait!

MACK. There's no time!

AMELIA *goes over to* JAYDEN, *who is still holding* SOMNA *at bay with the sword.*

AMELIA. You sure about this?

JAYDEN. Yeah.

SOMNA. THEN COVER YOUR EYES, BOY. STAY AND
　　DREAM.

MACK. Amelia, quick!

AMELIA (*to* JAYDEN). But I thought you hated me.

JAYDEN. No.

AMELIA. But why this? Why you?

JAYDEN. You'll work it out. One day. Now go.

　　AMELIA *hugs* JAYDEN.

　　The hourglass is almost empty.

MACK. Hurry!

SOMNA. COVER YOUR EYES.

JAYDEN (*to* AMELIA). Go!

　　JAYDEN *covers his eyes.*

　　AMELIA *joins the others.*

　　They pull back the curtains – light streams in.

　　SOMNA *dissolves back into the* NEVERBORN. *They*
　　scream as the light hits them.

NEVERBORN. NOOO!
　　DON'T LEAVE US HERE!
　　DON'T LEAVE UUUUUUSSSSS!!

　　The NEVERBORN *dissolve in the light and disappear,*
　　along with the dream world studio – and JAYDEN.

　　The others all wake up in bed, shielding the daylight from
　　their eyes.

　　JAYDEN *is not with them.*

　　The scene is exactly the same as at the start of the play,
　　except without the NEVERBORN. *They each take out a*
　　phone or laptop.

MADGE. Facebook: I'm awake. Who else is up? Share.

AMELIA. Me.

MACK. Me.

ALI. Me.

SURAYA. Too early, man. Share.

MADGE. I had mad dreams. Share.

RAPHAEL. Yeah and me! Share.

ALI. I saw the end of the world.

NASIMA. Me too.

MADGE. Yeah.

AMELIA. Yeah and me.

ALL. Yeah.

ALI. At least… that's what it felt like.

They meet up on the way to school.

BOYS. Alright.

GIRLS. Alright.

MACK. Did we all have the same dream?

AMELIA. Sounds like it.

MADGE. Sort of.

ALI. That's mad.

SURAYA. That totally freaks me out.

RAPHAEL. Yeah, and me.

NASIMA. I don't wanna think about it.

AMELIA. Yeah, let's just get to school.

MACK. You ready for this trip?

MADGE. Yeah, I guess.

MACK. What you bringing?

ALI. But when we get to school…

SURAYA. Where's the coach?

RAPHAEL. Where's our teachers?

NASIMA. Where's the trip?

MACK. That's weird.

AMELIA. We've definitely got the right day, right?

MADGE. Yeah.

ALI. Yeah.

SURAYA. Yeah.

MADGE. Well, we can't all be wrong.

ALI. Let's go and see miss.

TEACHER. Is this some sort of joke?

ALL. NO.

SURAYA. There was a school trip.

RAPHAEL. To Somna House.

NASIMA. Home of Charles Somna.

MACK. Inventor and movie pioneer.

AMELIA. Old guy.

MADGE. You must know him.

ALI. Invented the Somnagraph.

TEACHER. I have no idea what any of you are talking about.

ALL. BUT, MISS –

TEACHER. Now stop messing around and get to registration.

The bells go.

SURAYA. This is too weird.

RAPHAEL. I know.

NASIMA. I don't get it.

MACK. Did we dream all that? I mean, together?

AMELIA. That gives me the shivers.

MACK. Maybe when we were all online last night, we all fell asleep, and Facebook continued to connect us – even our dreams. Cos that's gotta at least be possible, right?

MADGE. I don't know, Mack.

ALI. You tell us.

SURAYA. We talked and talked.

RAPHAEL. And googled and googled.

NASIMA. But there never was a school trip.

MACK. There never was anyone called Charles Somna.

AMELIA. And Somna House, and the Somnagraph, never existed.

MADGE. At least, not outside of our dreams.

ALI. We still talk about it.

SURAYA. That strange night.

NASIMA. But as time streamed on.

MACK. Like grains of sand.

AMELIA. We talked about it less and less.

MADGE. And little by little.

RAPHAEL. We realise we're starting to grow up.

AMELIA takes out a few cans of Dr Pepper and hands them round to her friends.

AMELIA. I start to be a bit nicer, to value friendship, true friendship. Because that's where real riches are found.

MACK closes a textbook and puts his PSP away.

MACK. I start to accept that the more I study, the less I know. The universe is a big place. But on balance, there probably aren't giant lizards controlling everything. If anything, the real monsters are inside our heads. But the good news is, you can do something about those ones.

Someone chucks ALI *a football. He bounces it on the floor a couple of times.*

ALI. I start to obsess a bit less over business, though I'm still gonna study it at college. But now, I also look out for my mum, and take my little brother down the park to play football, every single day.

MADGE *opens an envelope containing her exam results.*

MADGE. I get an A-star in biology, and start to look into zoology courses at uni. Part of that is having to accept that death is part of nature, and we can't do anything about it. But I still campaign against slaughterhouses and battery farms, cos death might be natural, but it was never meant to be on a conveyor belt.

RAPHAEL *takes out an X-ray and looks at it.*

RAPHAEL. One day, at the hospital, I get some good news – the hole in my heart is naturally healing up as I grow. And overnight, for the first time, the clouds part, and I can start to see a future.

NASIMA *takes out a box of Fisherman's Friends.*

NASIMA. On my Auntie Zora's birthday, I get her a whole box of Fisherman's Friends. When she asks me why, I say, 'Because I love you.' And she takes me in her arms. 'You're young', she whispers, 'Don't abandon us just yet.' So I don't. Marriage, the army, both will always be there. But college comes first. Time to think. To learn. To live.

SURAYA *puts the stethoscope round her neck and takes out a medical textbook.*

SURAYA. As for me, I still haven't worked out a cure for insomnia. But I have started to use the time to study. And doctors hardly get any sleep, do they, so it's like the perfect career – I can do night shifts. Oh, and I worked out what the prawns mean. And no, I'm not gonna tell you. Work it out for yourself.

MACK. But there's one of us who'll never grow up.

AMELIA. He's also the one way we know we're not crazy.

MADGE. And that something did happen.

ALI. On that one, strange night last November.

SURAYA. We all remember Jayden.

RAPHAEL. But we're the only ones that do.

NASIMA. We hardly ever mention his name.

MACK. Not that it matters.

AMELIA. No one would know who we're talking about.

MADGE. Because it's like he never existed.

ALI. But every now and then, one of us dreams about him, and we'll tell the others.

AMELIA. I saw him last night.

RAPHAEL. Yeah?

AMELIA. Yeah. He was flying through space, chopping whole planets in half with a huge samurai sword.

NASIMA. That sounds like Jayden.

MACK. Yeah, man.

ALI. So he's doing alright then?

AMELIA. Seemed like it.

ALL. GOOD.

AMELIA. Yeah. He looked… happy.

RAPHAEL. Now, night-times are a bit less scary.

NASIMA. And dreams a safer place.

MACK. Because not only have we seen where they come from.

AMELIA. How they're made.

MADGE. And what they mean.

ALI. But each of us has our own personal guardian.

SURAYA. Watching over us.

RAPHAEL. To chase the nightmares away.

JAYDEN *appears in full ninja outfit.*

He busts a few moves with a wooden samurai sword.

He takes a long, slow bow.

The End.

FAST

Author's Note

Fast is set among a group of Year-Eleven classmates (fifteen to sixteen years old) of mixed social backgrounds, in a state secondary school, in a medium-sized British town, near to some countryside.

The play is written mostly naturalistically, except when Cara uses direct address to the audience. This is intended to set the scene quickly and allow the story to move quite easily through space and time – reducing the need for elaborate or detailed sets or scene changes. The scenes should flow into one another quite fluidly, without blackouts or lengthy set changes.

The play is intended to be performed with minimal decor and props. There is potential for the cast to act as an ensemble, physically and stylistically bringing some of the scenes to life. Exits/entrances can be interpreted loosely – they don't have to literally leave the stage but could just stand at the edge, or in neutral.

Fast was first performed as part of a young people's summer school run by Y Touring Theatre on 22 August 2014, with the following ensemble:

Shahel Ahmed
Johnny Collins
Malcom Couto
Imelda D'Souza
Kieran Ford
Ksanet Gebrehiwet
Chloe Johnson
Stephanie Lewis
Jeanelie Louamba
Aziz Malik
Makeda Maduka
Yasmin Nabavi

Directors	Dominique Poulter and Nathan Bryon
Designed by	The Company

Characters

CARA, *sixteen, lives on a farm outside town, rocks a sort of rural hippy look*

JAMES, *sixteen, young entrepreneur, works in Burger King but aspires to* The Apprentice

CHRIS, *sixteen, vegan eco-activist, his family home generates its own electricity*

SAFF, *fifteen, fast-food fan, overweight, lives with her dad who hates cooking*

SAJ, *fifteen, small, hyperactive, works in his dad's fried-chicken shop, addicted to energy drinks*

KASIA, *sixteen, athletic, serious, wants to be a chef, from a Polish family who own a grocer's*

ROB, *sixteen, sporty, outdoorsy, family all work in factories, deals contraband fizzy drinks in school*

HARRIET, *fifteen, articulate, academic, sits on the school council, Mum is an NHS nurse in the local hospital*

Older Characters

Note: These are all smaller parts. They can be played by individual actors, or one actor doubling all four, if necessary.

KIRSTY, *eighteen, Cara's older sister, hard-working, practical, wise beyond her years*

MISS CHILCOTT, *forties, the school headteacher, caring but firm, with a hint of steel*

CLAIRE BAINES, *thirties, journalist for the local* Herald *newspaper*

JULIETTE HANCOCK, *forties, elected councillor, constantly wired on coffee*

The cast are all onstage. They each hold a dictionary. CARA *talks directly to the audience.*

CARA. So it's lunchtime in school. Everyone's hungry. Except me. I don't get hungry. Not any more. It's summer term, exams are coming up, so they make us do these lunchtime revision classes. It's bullshit, they're not even about a subject, it's just words – literally going through the dictionary from A to Z. 'Five words a day,' Mr Perkins says – like fruit and veg. Like nutrients for the brain. All I know is it gives me a headache. Been doing it all year but we're still only on F.

Everyone opens their dictionaries to F. Moving down the column of words with their fingers, they read the words and definitions aloud.

ALL. Fffffff.

JAMES. 'Farouche – shy or ill at ease.'

CARA. 'Sullen or unsociable' mine says.

SAJ. Yeah, that sounds like you, Cara.

CARA. Shut up.

CHRIS. 'Farrier.'

SAFF. A what-ier?

KASIA. Fa-rr-ier.

ROB. Never heard of it.

KASIA. Me neither.

HARRIET. It's 'an expert in equine care'.

SAJ. You what?

CHRIS. Someone who looks after horses.

CARA. Don't you know anything?

SAJ. Yeah, alright, Farmer Girl, we're not all country bumpkins.

CHRIS. Cara's not a farmer, her dad is.

CARA. Was.

CHRIS. Yeah – sorry.

JAMES. 'Farrow – a litter of piglets.' I never knew that.

SAJ. Why would I wanna know that?

JAMES. I wonder what a tray of pork burgers would be?

HARRIET. A heart attack?

JAMES. About… forty quid profit I reckon.

SAFF. I don't touch pigs, innit.

SAJ. Yeah I don't think the pigs wanna be touched by you either, Saff.

SAFF. Pigs are dirty.

SAJ. The pigs are relieved.

ROB. 'Fart'!

SAJ. Eurgh – who?

ROB. No, it actually says fart – look!

SAFF. Oh my God it actually does.

SAJ. Brilliant!

CARA. Well, it is a word.

KASIA. But is it a proper word?

JAMES. It's in the dictionary.

ROB. 'To break wind from the anus'!

SAJ/ROB/JAMES. Ahahahahaha!

　　SAJ, ROB *and* JAMES *fall about laughing, then mimic farting.*

ROB. Excuse me while I break wind from my anus!

CARA. Oh, man.

CHRIS. That is so immature.

KASIA. Disgusting.

JAMES. Do you think 'shit' is in there?

SAJ. Yeah, look up shit.

HARRIET. We're on F.

ROB. I know an F-word.

CARA. Can we just get on with this?

CHRIS. Fart is also 'a worthless person' – says here.

HARRIET. Yeah, and 'to fart about – to waste time'.

SAJ. But mostly 'To break wind from the anus'!

ROB. I've gotta get that into the exam.

CHRIS. If you fart in the exam I will kill you.

JAMES. When nature calls, Chris.

CHRIS. Maybe you should change your diet.

SAJ. Maybe you should change your personality.

HARRIET. 'Fascinate – to interest exceedingly.'

KASIA. Exceedingly?

JAMES. *Exceedingly*, your honour.

SAJ. Your worship.

ROB. Your lordship.

JAMES. How very spiffing.

SAFF. Well, I ain't interested in this lesson.

ROB. Not even exceedingly?

SAFF. Not even a little bit. Can we go yet? I'm thirsty.

CARA. 'Fascism – authoritarian form of government characterised by extreme nationalism.'

SAJ/JAMES/ROB. Bor-ing.

SAFF. Sounds like this school.

KASIA. It's important *actually*, fascism caused millions of deaths in Europe last century.

JAMES. Yeah? Well, boredom's gonna cause millions of deaths in this school any minute.

SAFF. 'Fashion' – now you're talking.

SAJ. Pfff.

KASIA. 'The make or cut of a thing; vogue or trend.'

ROB. Yeah, and what would you two know about that?

KASIA. More than you – Lycra Boy.

SAFF. Yeah.

ROB. I ain't wearing Lyrca.

KASIA. I've seen you.

SAFF. Yeah, at the weekends.

KASIA. In your gimp outfit.

ROB. That's professional cycling gear, *actually*, you go faster in it.

SAFF. Like a horse?

ROB. You what?

SAFF. Getting whipped: Giddyup!

ROB. Shut up.

KASIA. Do your wax your chest and everything?

ROB. I don't need to.

SAJ. Why? Haven't you got no pubes?

ROB. It's not pubes on your chest, it's –

JAMES. What?

ROB. Man… hair… on the chest.

SAJ. Pubes.

ROB. Shut up.

JAMES. So have you got any or not?

HARRIET. Can someone please raise the tone of this conversation!

CHRIS. Seconded.

CARA. Ignore them.

CHRIS. Anyone'd think we're Year Sevens.

HARRIET. 'Fast – one: Able to move, function or take effect quickly.'

CHRIS. A fast horse.

HARRIET. A fast pain-reliever.

CARA. Gonna need one of them after this.

SAFF. A fast thinker.

ROB. So, not you then.

SAJ. 'Fast – two: Done in comparatively little time – fast food.'

ROB. Like your dad's chicken wings.

SAFF. Yeah, they're done in seconds.

JAMES. Time is money.

SAJ. They're cooked at a very high temperature.

SAFF. Then why are they always pink in the middle?

SAJ. They're not.

ROB. They are.

SAJ. They're not.

ALL. THEY ARE.

SAJ. It shows they're fresh!

CHRIS. Fresh out the freezer.

HARRIET. Yeah, it's cos they're half-raw.

SAJ. No they ain't.

ALL. THEY ARE.

SAJ. Well, you don't have to buy 'em!

CHRIS. I don't.

CARA. Nether do I.

HARRIET. Nor me – yuck.

JAMES. They're cheap.

KASIA. They're okay.

SAFF. Yeah, I love 'em.

CHRIS. I don't know how you lot can touch that stuff.

SAJ. Each to their own – weirdo.

ROB. Yeah, go and eat a carrot.

CHRIS. I'll tell you a good place for a carrot.

SAFF. Eurgh.

HARRIET. Can we stop talking about bodily things please?

JAMES. Who said anything about that?

CHRIS. Yeah, that's all in your imagination, Harriet.

HARRIET. Saff thought it too.

SAFF. Well, where would you put the carrot?

KASIA. In a salad?

CHRIS. Grated into hummus, mmmm.

SAJ. Yuck.

HARRIET. 'Fast – three: Stuck or sound – fast asleep.'

SAFF. Yeah that's me, zzzzzzzz.

CARA. 'Fast – four: In quick succession – events followed fast upon one another to the crisis.'

ROB. What crisis?

CARA. We're coming to that.

JAMES. 'Fast – five: Seeking excitement – sexually promiscuous'!

ROB/SAJ/JAMES. Oooooooh.

SAFF. 'A fast woman.' What does that mean?

JAMES. Not like you.

SAFF. I don't get that.

ROB. No, she's a *vast* woman, that's different.

SAJ/JAMES/KASIA. OOOOOOH!

SAFF. Yo, you want me to sit on you?

ROB. No thanks.

SAFF. Show you how vast I am.

CHRIS. That was below the belt, Rob.

CARA/HARRIET. Yeah.

SAFF (*to* ROB). Get on yer bike, freak.

ROB (*to* SAFF). I think you're the one that needs to do that.

SAJ/JAMES/KASIA. OOOOOOH!

CARA. Rob!

CHRIS. Don't rise to it, Saff.

HARRIET. Stop it, both of you! (*To* ROB.) Say sorry.

ROB. What for?

CARA. For being a dick.

HARRIET. For being nasty – for no reason.

SAFF. It's fine, I don't need his apology.

HARRIET. Well, he needs to give it.

JAMES. Jeez, man, sticks and stones.

CHRIS. Words hurt too.

HARRIET. Say it, Rob.

CARA. Yeah, say it.

   Pause.

ROB. Sorry.

HARRIET. Good.

CARA. Thank you.

HARRIET. What for?

SAJ. Enough already.

JAMES. Yeah, that'll do.

HARRIET. No, he needs to say what for. Rob?

ROB. It was just a joke.

SAFF. It's fine, whatever. Can't help my weight, can I?

ROB. Well –

CARA/HARRIET/CHRIS (*to* ROB). DON'T.

KASIA. 'Fast – six: To abstain from food completely.'

JAMES. To what from food?

KASIA. To stop eating.

JAMES. Oh. How long for?

KASIA. Doesn't say.

CHRIS. For a while.

HARRIET. For ages.

CARA. For ever.

SAFF. Nah, for a month.

JAMES. No, just for a day.

CHRIS. And a night – twenty-four hours.

SAFF. It's a month for us.

ROB. Who?

SAFF. Muslims.

SAJ. Do you go the whole month?

SAFF. Yeah.

SAJ. No you don't.

SAFF. 'Cept for iftar.[1]

SAJ. That don't count.

CARA. A fast can be as long as you want it to be.

JAMES. How about for an hour?

SAJ. No it has to be longer than that.

JAMES. Any longer's bad for business.

HARRIET. Anyway, it's good for you.

ROB. What, to starve yourself?

CHRIS. It's healthy, like a detox.

KASIA. I don't need a detox.

ROB. Yeah, my body's a temple.

HARRIET. Don't you mean a sewer?

ROB. I work it off.

HARRIET. On your gimp bike?

SAFF. Has anyone got any water?

HARRIET. Here. (*Sniffs*.) What's that smell?

SAFF. I dunno.

HARRIET. Kinda... fruity.

>   HARRIET *hands* SAFF *a bottle of water.* SAFF *drinks.*

>   MISS CHILCOTT *enters.*

KASIA. Shit, it's Miss Chilcott.

MISS CHILCOTT. I'll pretend I didn't hear that, Kasia. Alright, books down and listen up, please, class. Thank you for your time, I know you've got exams coming up. But as you know, tomorrow is the start of your twenty-four-hour fast for Oxfam. I'm pleased so many of you have signed up, and submitted your sponsorship forms. There's some impressive amounts pledged. Harriet, Cara, Chris – well done.

---

1. The Islamic name for breaking of the Ramadan fast after sundown each day.

KASIA (*mutters*). Creeps.

SAJ. Yeah, we can't all be rich.

MISS CHILCOTT. I'm sorry, Saj?

SAFF. Miss, does it have to be a whole twenty-four hours?

MISS CHILCOTT. Yes.

ROB. Why?

MISS CHILCOTT. Because that's what you've pledged to do.

SAFF. What about iftar?

MISS CHILCOTT. This is not a religious fast. It's for charity.

HARRIET. People in Africa go a lot longer than twenty-four little hours.

MISS CHILCOTT. That's right. It's all in a good cause. Now, I just need to give you some safety tips before you come in tomorrow.

JAMES. Miss, how will people know?

MISS CHILCOTT. Know what, James?

JAMES. That we haven't been eating.

SAJ. Cos you'll be all skinny.

HARRIET. Not after twenty-four hours.

MISS CHILCOTT. They'll just have to trust you. And you'll be expected to stick by your word. Those sponsorship forms are binding. Anyone caught eating without good reason *will* receive a detention.

SAFF. Miss, is being hungry a good reason?

MISS CHILCOTT. Don't be silly. You'll all be hungry, that's part of the experience. However, if you feel faint, or nauseous, or experience headaches, you *are* permitted to eat a small snack such as a biscuit.

SAFF. Just one?

MISS CHILCOTT. One or two. There will be an emergency supply in the school matron's office.

SAFF. What kind?

MISS CHILCOTT. I don't know.

SAFF. I only like Jammie Dodgers. And custard creams. And Bourbons. Oh, and those new Maryland Chunkies, mmm.

SAJ/JAMES/ROB. Mmmmm.

MISS CHILCOTT. I expect they'll be something plain like Rich Tea.

SAJ. Bleurgh.

JAMES. Yuck.

ROB. Boring.

MISS CHILCOTT. And if you get seriously ill, or actually pass out, your fast will be cancelled.

JAMES. Can we still claim our sponsorship money?

MISS CHILCOTT. No.

CHRIS. Course not, divvy, you've flunked out.

MISS CHILCOTT. That's right – they're paying you to go the full twenty-four hours. Anyone caught deliberately breaking the fast *will* be reported and their sponsors informed.

HARRIET. What about water?

MISS CHILCOTT. Thank you, Harriet, a very important point – all fluids are permitted. You may want to bring a sugary drink with you such as Lucozade.

ROB. Miss, I thought fizzy drinks was banned?

HARRIET. Yeah, they're unhealthy.

MISS CHILCOTT. Tomorrow will see a twenty-four-hour lifting of the school ban on fizzy drinks.

ROB. Result!

JAMES. Yessss!

CHRIS. No way!

HARRIET. Miss, that totally defeats the object!

ROB. It's not for health, it's for charideee.

HARRIET. Oh, like you care about that.

CARA. Yeah, Rob's gonna make a killing!

MISS CHILCOTT. It's just for one day. And, Rob, if I or any teacher catch you *selling* fizzy drinks in the playground –

ROB. I don't do that!

MISS CHILCOTT. – as we all know you do –

ROB. Prove it.

MISS CHILCOTT. – then you will spend the entire day –

ROB. That's slander, miss.

MISS CHILCOTT. – the entire day stood outside my office. Understood?

ROB. Yes, miss.

MISS CHILCOTT. That goes for all of you. Any questions?

ALL. Nooooo.

MISS CHILCOTT. Good. Thank you all once again for undertaking a charitable act.

SAFF. Can we go and get summing to eat now?

MISS CHILCOTT. Dismissed.

SAJ. Better go and stock up.

ROB. I could eat a horse.

SAFF. I could eat a farrier.

SAJ. A farrier's a person, you dick.

SAFF. I could still eat one. Still thirsty too. Harriet, you got any more water?

HARRIET. What, you finished it?

SAFF. Yeah.

SAJ (*to* SAFF). You have got the weirdest breath.

SAFF. Shut up.

They leave.

MISS CHILCOTT. Not you, Cara.

CARA. What have I done?

MISS CHILCOTT. Nothing.

MISS CHILCOTT *waits for the others to leave.*

How are you?

CARA. Fine.

MISS CHILCOTT. You sure?

CARA. Yeah.

MISS CHILCOTT. You don't have to do this, you know.

CARA. Why not?

MISS CHILCOTT. Because… grief can affect you physically.

CARA. I'm fine.

MISS CHILCOTT. It's only been a year.

CARA. Eleven months.

MISS CHILCOTT. Well, quite.

CARA. That's ages.

MISS CHILCOTT. No it's not. If you need to conserve your energy, your concentration, prioritise your exams –

CARA. I said I'm fine.

MISS CHILCOTT. Right. Alright. We're here for you, that's all I'm saying.

MISS CHILCOTT *goes.* CARA *turns to us.*

CARA. So it's the night before. Mum's away at another one of her spiritual-healing yoga retreats, so my big sister Kirsty cooks us dinner.

KIRSTY *and* CARA *open a dictionary each, which becomes a dinner plate. They take out a knife and fork from a compartment in the middle.* CARA *picks at her food but doesn't eat.*

KIRSTY. We had a viewing today.

Pause. CARA *doesn't answer.*

They were from a big chain. Industrial farming.

Pause.

The agent reckons they're serious.

Pause.

You should be pleased. If we can sell this place we might both get to go to uni.

CARA. One of the chickens has gone missing.

KIRSTY. Really? I don't know them all like you do.

CARA. It was Dad's favourite. The Amber White. The one with the red spot.

KIRSTY. You should eat.

CARA. I'm not hungry.

KIRSTY. Don't you like it?

CARA. No, I'm just not hungry.

KIRSTY. You're never hungry.

CARA. Can't help that, can I?

KIRSTY. You used to have a massive appetite.

CARA. Yeah, well, not any more.

KIRSTY. Tomorrow's the fast.

CARA. So?

KIRSTY. So you need to stock up.

CARA. Twenty-four hours is nothing.

KIRSTY. You'll be weak.

CARA. I've gone longer than that before.

KIRSTY. You've got revision.

CARA. Would you stop nagging me?

Pause.

KIRSTY. This asparagus is Dad's. He planted it. It takes three years to grow.

CARA *gets up.*

Where you going?

CARA. Upstairs.

She goes upstairs. She mimes opening a door and walking into a room.

(*To us.*) Mum and Dad's room's at the top of the house, looking out over the farm. Well, it's just Mum's room now. But Dad's wardrobe is still in the corner. Big. Solid. Like him.

CARA *opens the wardrobe.* [*Perhaps the rest of the cast could represent a large wardrobe with their dictionaries or bodies somehow.*]

Still full of his clothes.

CARA *takes out a large winter jumper. She pulls it over her head and puts it on. It is way too big. She hugs it to her.*

Still got his smell.

CARA *breathes it in. She cries.*

Miss him.

She gets angry.

But hate him.

She violently pulls the jumper off.

Miss him but hate him but miss him but hate him!

She flings the jumper into the wardrobe. It dislodges a shoebox which falls out. Letters spill onto the floor. She picks them up.

What the hell – ?

She reads some of them.

Oh my God.

KIRSTY *enters*.

KIRSTY. You alright?

CARA. Have you seen these?

KIRSTY. What are you doing in here?

CARA. Letters.

KIRSTY. Cara –

CARA. From Dad. From Dad to his clients.

KIRSTY. Look –

CARA. Tesco, Morrisons, Asda.

KIRSTY. Your dinner's getting cold.

    CARA *reads one of them out*.

CARA. 'Dear Asda head office, I enclose my farm's accounts
for the last financial year. As you will see, for the third year
running, it made a heavy loss, driving my business further
into debt – '

KIRSTY. Cara –

CARA. 'Your company's "price promise" to customers does not
appear to be coming out of your profits. It is coming out of
mine.'

KIRSTY. Alright, Cara, just stop.

CARA. There's hundreds of them –

KIRSTY. It's private.

CARA. To all the supermarkets he supplied.

KIRSTY. It's just old work letters.

CARA. Stretching back years –

KIRSTY. You shouldn't have read them.

CARA. He's dead, Kirsty.

KIRSTY. Then all the more reason!

CARA. But they all say the same thing! 'I'm struggling', 'You're driving me into debt', 'I've got two daughters who want to go to university'.

KIRSTY. Farming's hard –

CARA. Not this hard.

KIRSTY. – everyone knows that.

CARA. But this is why he did it, Kirsty! This is why he killed himself!

Pause.

KIRSTY. We don't know that, Cara. Nobody does. That's what happens when they don't leave a note.

CARA (*of the letters*). Well, maybe this is his note.

KIRSTY. Come down. Eat your dinner.

CARA. You know what? I never want to eat again.

CARA storms off. KIRSTY flicks through the letters.

Several bedside alarms go off.

The rest of the cast come on, yawning.

ROB. I'm starving.

JAMES. Yeah, and me.

CHRIS. It's horrible.

SAFF. Like a black hole in my belly.

SAJ. It's only breakfast time.

KASIA. Yeah, get a grip, you've got all day left.

HARRIET. Why is the school canteen open?

ALL. Yeah!

ROB. Man, that is just cruel.

JAMES. It's empty.

SAFF. It's taunting us.

HARRIET. That is such a waste of food – who's gonna buy it?

ROB. Anyone want any Lucozade?

SAFF. Yeah, me.

SAJ. Yeah, give us some.

JAMES. I'll have one.

KASIA. Yeah, go on then.

HARRIET. Wait, are you selling this?

ROB. Nope. There's a hire charge though.

KASIA. For what?

ROB. Holding the bottle.

HARRIET. That is selling it!

CHRIS. Yeah!

ROB. No it's not, it's a hire charge!

JAMES. What – am I gonna sick it back up? Return it?

ROB. I don't need the Lucozade back, just the bottle.

SAJ. How much?

ROB. Quid for twenty minutes.

SAFF. Done.

HARRIET. You are so wrong.

SAFF, KASIA, SAJ and JAMES each give ROB a pound in exchange for a Lucozade.

The school bell goes. CARA slopes in quietly.

KASIA. Maths.

CHRIS. Urgh, double maths.

ROB. First thing too.

SAFF. They should just cancel everything.

SAJ. Yeah, we ain't gonna get anything done.

They open their maths exercise books.

HARRIET. 'A farmer has to stock his new farm and has allocated one hundred pounds to purchase livestock.'

CHRIS. Why can't it be a vegetable farm?

SAJ. Shut up, freak.

CARA. Only one hundred pounds? That's stupid.

HARRIET. 'The eagerly awaited day arrives when he is able to attend market.'

CHRIS. He? What if it's a female farmer?

CARA. Yeah.

JAMES. Right on.

HARRIET. 'He discovers that horses cost ten pounds each.'

ROB. Only a tenner?

JAMES. In that case I'll have two.

HARRIET. 'Ducks are eight for one pound.'

CARA. Pfff.

SAJ. In that case I'll have eighty.

SAFF. No one eats ducks.

SAJ. The Chinese do – fry 'em up.

HARRIET. ' – and sheep are one pound each.'

CARA. That's ridiculous.

ROB. Hang on, why is everything about food?

JAMES. Yeah, are they doing this deliberately?

KASIA. I'm too hungry to think.

SAFF. I'm too thirsty.

CHRIS. It's not about food, it's about animals.

SAJ. Yeah, food.

CHRIS. You don't have to eat animals. You could use them for wool, or feathers.

SAJ. Or kebabs.

JAMES/ROB/SAJ/SAFF. Mmmm, kebabs.

HARRIET. 'Help the farmer calculate what combination of each animal he could buy to meet his target of exactly one hundred animals while spending all of his budget.'

JAMES. Easy. Seven horses, twenty sheep, eighty ducks.

KASIA. You what?

ROB. I didn't know we had Carol Vorderman[2] in class.

SAFF. Swot.

JAMES. It's just maths. But the more important question is: what's the profit?

HARRIET. There are other things in life too, you know.

JAMES. Yeah? Like what?

School bell.

HARRIET. English lit.

ROB. Oh, man, please not English.

HARRIET. I love English.

CHRIS. Yeah, all those books.

CARA. Gotta pick one for the exam.

JAMES. *Like Water for Chocolate.*

SAJ. *Oranges Are Not the Only Fruit.*

SAFF. *The Particular Sadness of Lemon Cake.*

KASIA. Why are they all about food?!

ROB. Someone is definitely doing this deliberately!

SAFF. I am so hungry it's not even funny.

School bell.

HARRIET. Lunchtime.

SAFF. Yo, what is the point of lunch?

ROB. Yeah, they should cancel it.

JAMES. Do a lesson instead.

2. If this reference dates the play, it can be substituted with any well-known figure who is good at maths, either contemporary or historical, e.g. Albert Einstein.

SAJ. Take our minds off it.

KASIA. Yeah, I have to do something to forget this hunger.

SAFF (*to* ROB). Can I get another Lucozade?

ROB *sells her one*.

CHRIS. Dictionaries!

HARRIET. Brilliant idea!

CHRIS. Five words a day.

HARRIET. Where we up to?

CARA. G.

ALL. G G G G.

ROB. 'Galia – a type of melon.'

JAMES. 'Ganache – a mixture of chocolate and cream.'

CHRIS. 'Garibaldi – biscuit with a layer of currants.'

SAFF. 'Garlic.'

SAJ. 'Gherkin.'

KASIA. 'Ginger.'

HARRIET. Oh, this is torture!

They throw the dictionaries down.

Let's talk instead.

ALL. Okay.

They all get out their smartphones and start tapping at them.

SAJ. I found a chicken.

ROB. You what?

HARRIET. I don't wanna talk about food.

CHRIS. It isn't food, it's a chicken.

CARA. What d'you mean you 'found it'?

SAJ. In my back yard.

ROB. What – of the chicken shop?

SAJ. Yeah.

CARA. What – alive?

SAJ. Yeah, it just flew in.

JAMES. A chicken flew into the back yard of your chicken shop?

SAJ. Yeah.

ROB. Was it suicidal?

SAJ. It did look a bit sad.

KASIA. Did you kill it?

SAJ. No, it's still there.

CARA. Where?

SAJ. I put it in a box.

CHRIS. That's cruel.

SAFF. That's free meat.

JAMES. Yeah, what's the profit on one chicken?

SAJ. Pfff, not nearly enough.

CARA. Leave it alone.

SAJ. What?

CARA. Whatever you do, you don't touch that chicken. Understand?

ROB. Whoa. Easy, tiger.

HARRIET. PLEASE can we stop talking about food?

School bell.

KASIA. Oh thank God.

HARRIET. Design and technology.

JAMES. Should be safe with that.

ROB. Mock exam: food technology.

ALL. NOOOOOO!

SAFF. 'Write a short essay describing the influence that Gordon Ramsay[3] has had on the cooking and presentation of food.'

SAJ. This is a sick joke, right?

KASIA. Gordon Ramsay's my hero.

CHRIS. He's horrible.

HARRIET. Yeah, I hate him.

KASIA. Everyone hates chefs, that's part of the job.

SAJ. Is that why everyone hates you?

KASIA. You should see me in the kitchen.

SAFF. 'Include Ramsay's opinions in relation to home cooking.' What's 'home cooking'?

CHRIS. What your dad doesn't do.

SAFF. Yo, shut up about my dad.

JAMES. I can feel a big, fat F-word coming on.[4]

ROB. Yeah, and it ain't 'food'.

HARRIET. Wait, the next one's easier. 'Fill in the blanks in the following sentence. "Reducing the amount of" – '

ALL. FAT.

HARRIET. "– you consume can prevent heart-related diseases. If you reduce your intake of – "

ALL. SUGAR.

HARRIET. " – it can help prevent" – '

ALL. DIABETES.

HARRIET. Very good.

SAFF. I scored zero.

HARRIET. Did you know we share sixty per cent of our DNA with a banana?

---

3. If this reference dates the play, it can be substituted with any contemporary celebrity chef.
4. If the Gordon Ramsay reference is changed, this line and the next can be cut.

CHRIS. Really? Why?

HARRIET. I have no idea. Not even Miss Myles in science can tell me.

SAFF. What about a potato?

ROB. You share a hundred per cent DNA with that.

SAFF. Shut up.

School bell.

Oh my God I'm gonna die.

SAJ. Is that thunder?

SAFF. That's my stomach.

JAMES. I feel sick.

CHRIS. You can eat biscuits if you feel sick.

JAMES. But what about my sponsors?

SAFF. Yeah, think of the kids, man.

A longer school bell – to signify the end of the day.

ROB. Home time!

SAFF. At last!

ALL. MUUUM?! What's for dinner?!

They all leave, except for CARA. KIRSTY *comes on with another meal.*

KIRSTY. Twenty-four hours. Well done. I did your favourite.

CARA. Not hungry.

KIRSTY. You must be.

CARA. No.

KIRSTY. Car, come on. This isn't healthy.

CARA. Who said anything about health?

KIRSTY. Alright, I get it. You're angry. You've made your point. Now eat.

CARA. I haven't even started to make my point.

CARA *pushes her food away.*

KIRSTY. Where you going?

CARA. Out.

CARA *walks.*

She gets to SAJ*'s chicken shop.* SAJ *is at the counter wearing a hat and a uniform.*

SAJ. Next! (*Sees* CARA.) Oh, hi.

CARA. Alright.

SAJ. You never come in here.

CARA. I don't want your food.

SAJ. Fine, all the more for us. Next!

CARA. Does your dad make you wear that?

SAJ. If you're not buying, can you move aside?

CARA. I'm here for my chicken.

SAJ. I thought you said –

CARA. Not dead, cooked, fried chicken. The live one. In your back yard.

SAJ. Oh, that.

CARA. It's still there, right? You haven't killed it?

SAJ. Nah. It's kinda cute.

CARA. It's my dad's.

SAJ. How do you know that?

CARA. It escaped.

SAJ. Don't they all look the same?

CARA. That's racist.

SAJ. Chickens aren't a race.

CARA. This one has a red spot – right?

SAJ. …Maybe.

CARA. It's called an Amber White.

SAJ. You've given it a name?

CARA. It's a breed. Hand it over.

SAJ. It looks more like that pop star to me. What's-her-name. The one off *The Voice*.[5]

CARA. Just hand it over, Saj.

SAJ. Oh like I've got it in my back pocket.

CARA. I'll wait.

SAJ. I'm busy. Next!

CARA. I'm not moving.

SAJ. You're holding up the queue.

CARA. Let them wait.

SAJ. Cara, these people are hungry.

CARA. Let them wait. (*Turns to queue.*) You can wait a bit longer, can't you? For your greasy, fried, dead shit.

SAJ. Oi! You can't come in here and talk to our customers like that.

CARA (*to queue*). Your lifeless, battery-farmed lumps of fat.

SAJ. Don't make me get my dad.

CARA. Go and get him.

SAJ. Cara, you're being weird.

CARA. No, go and get him. Because it's people like him, and places like this, which killed *my* dad!

SAJ. What?!

CARA *runs out.*

(*To next customer.*) Sorry about that. What can I get you? Chicken bucket? Nice choice.

CARA *knocks on a door.* CHRIS *opens it. He is eating a celery stick dipped in a tub of hummus.*

5. Reference can be updated if necessary.

CHRIS. Oh, Cara, hi.

CARA. Put that down. We need to talk.

CHRIS. About what?

CARA. Get your phone out.

CHRIS. Why?

CARA. I want you to film me.

CHRIS. What's this about?

CARA. A new campaign. I think you'll like it.

> CHRIS *gets out his phone and opens the camera app.* CARA *paces.*

CHRIS. What's it about? We're never gonna get the school canteen to go vegan, you know. Or even veggie I reckon. Did you know that the manager of the Turkey Twiglet factory in town is a school governor? My mum found that out. It's a complete stitch-up. They'll be sponsoring sports day next. It's no different to McDonald's and the Olympics.

CARA. Just hit record.

> *He starts recording.* CARA *speaks to camera.*

(*To camera.*) My name is Cara Leary. I'm in Year Eleven at Redford Secondary. Twenty-four hours ago I stopped eating. It was a sponsored fast for Oxfam, but I've decided to make it last. Twelve months ago, my dad lay down on some train tracks in the middle of the night. He was a farmer. For years he'd been screwed by the big supermarkets and fast-food chains who refused to pay him a proper price for his crops.

My dad was a quiet man, and never spoke about this. But I'm not quiet. And this is my protest. I will not be eating again until Redford Secondary bans all snack machines on school premises. I will not be eating again until Redford Secondary uses only fairly traded UK produce in its canteen. I will not eat again until our local council clamps down on the thirty-seven fast-food outlets that exist within one square mile of our school. And I will not eat again until I get meetings with heads of all the major supermarket chains which have an outlet in our town. This fast started for charity. But charity begins at home. Join me, and help demand a living wage for UK farmers and their families. Enough is enough. The revolution starts here.

CHRIS stops filming.

CHRIS. Shit. You sure about this?

CARA. Surer then I've ever been.

CHRIS. It's like a – a hunger strike.

CARA. You bet. Are you in?

CHRIS. I don't know. I've just eaten some celery.

CARA. Celery doesn't count, it's mostly water.

CHRIS. Mum's cooking dinner.

CARA. Tell her you don't need it.

CHRIS. I'm starving.

CARA. So are British farmers. This is it, Chris. You talk the talk, about food, the environment, ethics. You're an eco-warrior, you said so yourself. It's time to step up.

CHRIS. Alright. Let's do it. I'm in.

CARA. Thanks, mate. (*Points to his phone.*) We need to get that onto YouTube.

CHRIS starts to upload the film. The rest of the cast all open their laptops [maybe the dictionaries double up?] and watch the film. If a screen is available it would be nice to see a bit of it.

JAMES. Shit.

ROB. Oh my God.

SAFF. Cara, you nutter.

HARRIET. Wicked.

KASIA. She's gonna kill herself.

SAJ. I'm gonna kill *her*.

They close their laptops and cluster round CARA.

HARRIET. You need to add a health angle – cheap, processed food is the leading cause of obesity and heart disease.

CHRIS. You need to talk about the environment – industrial farming causes massive pollution.

SAJ. She needs to shut up – this is such a stupid idea.

HARRIET. Why?

KASIA. Well, maybe some of us want drinks and snacks in school.

JAMES. Yeah, it's the free market, man, you can't stop it.

SAJ. You've no right to do this – those takeaways are family businesses.

ROB. Yeah, and I can sell whatever I want in the playground.

HARRIET. Oh, so you admit you're a calorie salesman.

ROB. Calories are fine so long as you work them off.

HARRIET. We can't all be Bradley Wiggins.[6]

SAJ. Hey, you know how they break a hunger strike in Guantanamo, don't you?

SAJ/JAMES/ROB. Force-feeding!

CARA. Piss off.

The boys advance on CARA *with sandwiches, crisps and chocolate bars drawn as weapons.*

Get away from me!

JAMES. Open wide!

CHRIS. This is serious!

Only SAFF *is quiet, standing away from the throng. She reads a medical pamphlet.* MISS CHILCOTT *enters.*

MISS CHILCOTT. Alright, that's enough! Get out of here, all of you. Cara, Chris: my office, now.

MISS CHILCOTT'*s office.* CARA *and* CHRIS *stand sulkily.*

Do you want to tell me what all this is about?

---

6. If this dates the play any famous cyclist can be substituted here.

CHRIS. It's all in the video.

MISS CHILCOTT. Yes, which is going round the entire school. Do you want to put our students in danger?

CARA. What's dangerous?

MISS CHILCOTT. Exams are coming up, people are trying to revise.

CARA. They can drink energy drinks.

MISS CHILCOTT. Full of caffeine, which puts stress on the heart.

CARA. Ginger beer then. Ginger's a natural stimulant.

CHRIS. Actually, ginger beer is eighty per cent sugar, Cara.

CARA. No one has to fast with me.

MISS CHILCOTT. You're encouraging them to.

CARA. People can think for themselves.

MISS CHILCOTT. You're the oldest in the school now, Cara. Younger students look up to you.

CHRIS. You're the ones who started it all with this fast.

MISS CHILCOTT. For charity, Chris, not for this.

CHRIS. What's the difference?

MISS CHILCOTT. In fact, Chris, could you wait outside?

CHRIS *sighs and leaves*.

Look. I know this is about your dad. We're all really, really sorry. You're grieving. It's understandable. But he wouldn't have wanted this.

CARA. How do you know what he would've wanted?

MISS CHILCOTT. Cara, we will support you in every way we can to get through this difficult period in your life. But if you choose to harm yourself then that's a different matter.

CARA. I'm not harming myself.

MISS CHILCOTT. That's what a hunger strike is.

CARA. I'll tell you what's harmful. Industrial farming. Low-cost, high-calorie food that strangles farmers and slowly kills consumers. Thirty-seven fast-food outlets within one mile of school, snack machines in every school corridor –

MISS CHILCOTT. We've banned fizzy drinks.

CARA. And what about the crisps, chocolate, biscuits – right by the tills in the school canteen?

MISS CHILCOTT. Alright, we can look at that.

CARA. Really? How?

MISS CHILCOTT. How about instead of starving yourself, you get a petition together. See how many signatures you can gather. I'll take it to the school governors.

CARA. Too long.

MISS CHILCOTT. What's the hurry?

CARA. I'm fasting.

MISS CHILCOTT. Then stop.

CARA. Remove the snack machines.

MISS CHILCOTT. How about we reduce their number?

CARA. All of them. Now.

MISS CHILCOTT. I'll take a proposal to the governors to remove half.

CARA. All of them.

MISS CHILCOTT. Two-thirds.

CARA. You can keep one.

MISS CHILCOTT. Will you start eating again?

CARA. I'll need to talk to my campaign manager.

MISS CHILCOTT. Cara –

CARA. There's also the canteen menu.

MISS CHILCOTT. That's a whole different matter.

CARA. Did you know that Comida Limited, who provide our school meals, is part of the biggest industrial-farming corporation in Europe?

School bells go.

MISS CHILCOTT. It's lunchtime. I have a staff meeting. Go and eat something.

MISS CHILCOTT *goes.* CHRIS *is waiting.*

CHRIS. How'd it go?

CARA. We've got the power. We just need a few more of us.

HARRIET *comes over.*

HARRIET. I'm in.

CHRIS. Wicked.

CARA. Nice one, Harriet.

HARRIET. My mum's a nurse, she sees the effects of this all the time. Obesity costs billions.

CHRIS. Yeah, and it's the public picks up the tab, never McDonald's.

CARA. We need to write a manifesto.

HARRIET. Great idea.

CARA. And a list of demands.

CHRIS. I'll get onto it.

CARA. You should've seen Miss Chilcott's face. I reckon we can push her for more.

HARRIET. More what?

CHRIS. Remove chips from the canteen.

CARA. Yeah, proper prices paid for quality ingredients from British farmers.

CHRIS. Organic fruit at break times.

CARA. Home economics back on the curriculum.

CHRIS. Round up the playground snack-dealers.

HARRIET. Where does it all end?

CARA. I'm only just getting started. It's the council next.

HARRIET. School council?

CARA. Town council. We need to access the corridors of power.

SAFF comes over, clutching her leaflet. She looks a bit in shock.

CHRIS. Hey, Saff, are you in on this hunger strike?

SAFF. I've got diabetes.

CHRIS. What?

CARA. Shit, man.

SAFF. I've just found out.

HARRIET. Oh, Saff.

SAFF. I fainted yesterday. Went to the doctor. I've gotta have tests, but I've got all the symptoms: fruity breath, constantly thirsty, fainting…

CARA. Can you still fast?

HARRIET. Cara!

CARA. What?

HARRIET. It might not be safe.

SAFF. I'll check. But I will if I can. Gotta lose weight anyway now, haven't I? I can't believe this…

HARRIET. It's not your fault.

SAFF. I know. It's the fast-food companies innit. All that junk they put in.

CHRIS. That's right.

HARRIET. Well… it is lifestyle too, Saff.

CHRIS. Harriet.

HARRIET. Sorry, but it's true. Lack of exercise is just as important.

SAFF. Yeah. I know.

HARRIET. See?

CHRIS. But –

HARRIET. Someone's gotta say it, Chris.

SAFF. I know, I gotta sort it out. I don't wanna die.

CHRIS. Hey, you're not gonna die.

CARA. We're all gonna die.

CHRIS. Alright, Grim Reaper, you know what I mean.

SAFF. Anyway, count me in.

CARA. Good girl.

HARRIET. Yeah.

CHRIS. I'll teach you some recipes if you like.

CARA. I hope you like celery.

CHRIS. And yoga.

SAFF. I'll – I'll give it a try.

HARRIET. And I'll help with the medical stuff. Look it over.

SAFF. Aw, I love you guys.

> SAFF *cries. The others comfort her.* ROB *enters.*

ROB. What's the matter – canteen run out of chips?

CARA/CHRIS/HARRIET. Shut up, Rob.

> CHRIS *takes out his phone and presses record.* CARA, HARRIET *and* SAFF *line up in front of it.* HARRIET *distributes some banners. They say things like:*

> *'Tescos: Pulling a Fast One.'*

> *'Fasting against Fast Food.'*

> *'Fasting for Farmers.'*

> ROB, JAMES, KASIA *and* SAJ *gather to watch them. They are not impressed.*

CHRIS (*Geordie accent, to camera*). Day two.

CARA. It's not *Big Brother*.

CHRIS. Sorry. (*Without accent*.) Day two.

CARA. Actually it's day three for me, if you count the original twenty-four hours for Oxfam.

SAFF. I had a burger that night.

HARRIET. Yeah, that resets the clock.

CHRIS. Day two slash three. The hunger strikers are now four in number.

CARA. We've still touched nothing but water and orange juice.

HARRIET. Feeling a bit sick actually.

CHRIS. Yeah, weird feeling in my guts.

SAFF. Yeah, stomach cramps and acid burps.

HARRIET. Too much information.

CARA. But we're hanging in there.

CHRIS/SAFF/HARRIET. Yeah.

CHRIS. Join us on Facebook.

HARRIET. Group name: 'Pulling a Fast One.'

CHRIS. Follow us on Twitter.

CARA. Hashtag: Fast.

CHRIS. View our protest banners on Tumblr.

SAFF. And join us at lunchtime every day this week outside –

CHRIS/SAFF/HARRIET/CARA. Tesco on the high street.

SAFF. For some plate-smashing action.

HARRIET. One for every meal we've missed.

They each smash a plate on the floor.[7]

CHRIS. Right, these are our demands.

CARA. We want a meeting with the local council.

CHRIS. And with the heads of Tesco.

---

7. Not strictly necessary if budget is limited or being performed in an enclosed space!

HARRIET. And Morrisons.

CARA. And Sainsbury's.

SAFF. And Asda.

CHRIS. And Waitrose.

HARRIET. I thought Waitrose was alright?

CARA. Yeah, they charge more so they pay more to farmers.

SAFF. Anyway, whatever.

CHRIS. Demand one: the local council converts all spare land to vegetable patches.

HARRIET. Demand two: free cookery classes in all schools and community centres.

SAFF. Demand three: fast food to have warnings on it, like cigarettes, with all massive fat people on it.

CARA. Demand four: all supermarkets to publish the percentage which goes to the farmer next to the price of every product.

JAMES. This is bullshit.

ROB/SAJ. Yeah.

CARA. What?

JAMES. You're a bunch of do-gooders.

CHRIS. What's wrong with that?

KASIA. Telling everyone else what to do.

HARRIET. Why don't you join us rather than sniping from the sidelines?

JAMES. Because you haven't got a clue.

CARA. About what?

JAMES. About anything.

CARA. I know about farming.

HARRIET. I know about the NHS – my mum's a nurse.

SAFF. Yeah, and I know about diabetes.

CHRIS. I know about the environment.

ROB. So?

CARA. So which part of that is 'bullshit'?

SAJ. All of it.

JAMES. Yeah, people want it.

CARA/HARRIET/CHRIS. So?

JAMES. So give it to them.

CARA. They shouldn't be able to have it.

CHRIS. Yeah.

ROB. Oh, what, you're gonna ban fast food?

CHRIS. We ban drugs.

JAMES. This is nothing like drugs.

HARRIET. Why? They both cause harm.

ROB. So do booze and fags.

HARRIET. Yes, and we should ban those.

KASIA. Would you listen to yourselves?

JAMES. Worthies.

ROB. Food fascists.

KASIA. Who are you to tell us what to do?

CARA. Kasia, you work in a grocer's.

KASIA. Yeah, an affordable one.

CHRIS. Don't you care about pesticides and air miles?

KASIA. Not really.

HARRIET. But you wanna be a chef!

KASIA. So?

HARRIET. So don't you wanna cook healthy food?

KASIA. I'll cook whatever people pay me to cook.

CHRIS. Well, someone's got to take a stand.

ROB. You can afford to.

HARRIET. What's that supposed to mean?

ROB. 'Waitrose is fine' – Jesus.

CHRIS. Waitrose *is* fine.

ROB. Waitrose costs three times the money!

KASIA. You're a bunch of rich kids.

JAMES. Yeah, some people can't afford proper food.

SAFF. I'm not rich.

ROB. No, you're easily led.

SAFF. Piss off.

CHRIS. Anyway, vegetables are cheap.

ROB. Not from Waitrose they ain't.

JAMES. But veg doesn't fill you up.

CHRIS. Yeah it does.

ROB. Yeah, if you're a scrawny vegan.

CHRIS. Shut up.

SAJ. Real men eat meat.

CHRIS. Real men care about the planet.

JAMES. I care about the planet – about how much money I can make out of it.

ROB. If you work two jobs, like my mum, there ain't no time to cook!

CARA. *You* could cook!

ROB. I'm a bloke!

JAMES. It's about freedom!

KASIA. That's right!

JAMES. People are free to do what they like to their bodies – it's no one else's business!

HARRIET. It is if costs us all money!

ROB. How does it do that?

HARRIET. Through the NHS!

CARA. Yeah, we all pay for that through our taxes!

JAMES. Then so do all the fat people!

ROB. Yeah, they're entitled to the treatment they've paid for!

Everyone shouts at once.

CLAIRE BAINES enters.

CLAIRE. Excuse me!

The shouting stops.

Which one of you is Cara Leary?

CARA. That's me.

CLAIRE. Could I have a word?

The others leave. CLAIRE holds out her hand.

Claire Baines. I'm from the *Herald*. I've heard about your campaign. Can I ask you a few questions?

CLAIRE takes out a voice recorder.

CARA. Sure. What do you want to know?

CLAIRE. Why don't we start at the start?

CARA. Alright. It started with these. Letters from my dad.

CARA takes out the letters from her dad.

We segue into another scene: CLAIRE exits and KIRSTY enters, reading from an open copy of the Herald.

KIRSTY. 'Local school student Cara Leary is a girl on a mission. Inspired by a twenty-four-hour charity fast at school, the sixteen-year-old has vowed not to eat again until the heads of Tesco and the local council meet with her. The campaign is a bid to draw attention to the effect on British farmers of a decade of supermarket price wars, which Leary blames for driving her late father into a spiral of debt which eventually resulted in his suicide – as evidenced by a moving collection of letters which she showed our reporter.'

KIRSTY *throws the paper at* CARA.

Those letters were private!

CARA. They're evidence.

KIRSTY. You should never have taken them out of his room.

CARA. People have to know.

KIRSTY. Mum's gonna kill you.

CARA. Mum doesn't even notice us any more, Kirsty.

KIRSTY. That's not true.

CARA. Yeah it is. This family's falling apart.

KIRSTY. Well, you're not helping!

CARA. And there's nothing either of us can do to stop it.

KIRSTY. Your dinner's in the dog.

CARA. Good. I'm fasting, aren't I?

KIRSTY *storms out.*

CHRIS *enters.*

CHRIS. Um, Cara? Someone called Juliette Hancock just rang.

CARA. Who's that?

CHRIS. A local councillor. She said she's standing for election.

She wants to talk to you.

JULIETTE HANCOCK *bustles in, holding two takeaway coffees.*

She talks very fast.

JULIETTE. Ah, you must be Cara, good good, come in, come in. I've heard all about your campaign, it's excellent, really excellent, as is your timing.

CARA. Really?

JULIETTE. Yes, elections are coming up, don't you read the papers? I've won the past three and been a major part of this borough's decision-making for the best part of a decade, I've always got my ear to the ground for local issues.

CARA. Oh, I see.

JULIETTE. Coffee?

CARA. Er, no thanks.

JULIETTE. Good for you, filthy habit, makes you smell. I drink ten cups a day.

   JULIETTE *downs one of the coffees and starts drinking the other.*

CARA. Right, er –

JULIETTE. So, you and I have a lot to offer each other. You're absolutely right that there's far too many fast-food outlets in this town, far too many, especially around the schools, and with obesity out of control, something needs to be done. Well, I've decided that I'm the one to do it.

CARA. Right, great, but this is also about Tescos and what they pay farmers –

JULIETTE. Of course it is, of course it is, but Tescos are also a major local employer, we have to remember that.

CARA. Oh.

JULIETTE. Whereas the fast-food outlets, what do they do for us? Not much, I can tell you. They stink out the town, make us all fat, leave their rubbish and grease all over the pavements, only employ immigrants and attract nothing but drunks. Something needs to be done.

CARA. What about Tesco?

JULIETTE. One step at a time.

CARA. Right.

JULIETTE. Let's deal with the manageable problem first, shall we? Now. I'll back your campaign and pledge to enact new by-laws if you'll publicly endorse my stand for re-election.

CARA. What does that mean?

JULIETTE. Just a few photos, standing next to me outside some chicken and kebab shops –

JULIETTE *poses next to* CARA*, someone takes a photo. Perhaps it could appear on a screen somewhere.*

– thumbs up, big smile – and maybe a quote for my leaflets.

CARA. Er, okay.

Someone takes notes while JULIETTE *dictates.*

JULIETTE. 'I'm thrilled to have the support of highly respected local councillor Juliette Hancock, in my campaign – *our* campaign – to clamp down on the scurrilous scourge of the purveyors of junk food in our local area. Cease the Grease!'

CARA. Actually the campaign slogan is 'Pulling a Fast One' –

JULIETTE. Tell you what, I could bring my team to your family's farm, have some shots taken in the fields, maybe digging a hole, planting some trees –

Someone hands JULIETTE *a spade, she poses for another photo.*

– yes, the farming community are very politically active.

CARA. My farm grows vegetables, not trees –

JULIETTE. Fantastic, fantastic, so we have a deal?

JULIETTE *holds out her hand. More photos.*

CARA. Erm, alright, I think so.

JULIETTE. Marvellous! Right, I'm off to open a community centre then got a road protest on the bypass at three followed by a maternity-ward photo shoot and a 'best-kept pub garden' award, got to dash!

JULIETTE *goes.*

The others enter all holding one of JULIETTE*'s campaign leaflets with* JULIETTE *and* CARA *featured on the front, along with the slogan 'Cease the Grease'.*

CHRIS. They're wheeling away the snack machines.

HARRIET. Hurrah!

SAFF. The canteen's stopped doing chips.

HARRIET. And burgers.

JAMES. And pizza.

SAFF. And lasagne.

ROB. I just got suspended for selling lemonade!

KASIA. I need chocolate to concentrate on revising!

JAMES. It's the nanny state gone mad.

> SAJ *comes in carrying a box with something inside.*
>
> *He slams it down then marches up to* CARA, *brandishing one of* JULIETTE's *leaflets.*
>
> SAFF, HARRIET *and* CHRIS *block his way.*

SAJ. Withdraw your backing for that crazy councillor.

CHRIS. She can't do that, Saj.

SAJ (*jostling* CHRIS). Out of my way, vegan.

HARRIET. Just calm down.

SAJ. She's gonna pass by-laws which will close us down!

HARRIET. Good.

SAJ. Limits on how many chicken shops, how close to schools, the hours we can open.

SAFF. I'm sad too.

CHRIS. But something had to be done.

SAJ. The bottom's gonna drop out of the market!

HARRIET. That's the idea.

SAJ. These are small businesses, legitimate family firms –

CHRIS. Find another trade.

SAJ. Like what? Tofu farmer?

CHRIS. You don't grow tofu, you make it.

SAJ. You can shove it up your arse for all I care. Let me talk to Cara.

HARRIET. She's busy right now.

SAJ. Cara – I've got your dad's chicken.

CARA. What?

Clucking comes from inside the box.

SAJ. The one what flew into my back yard.

SAJ *takes out a cheese wire.*

Have you ever killed a chicken?

CARA. Don't you dare.

SAJ. It's easy. All you need's a wire.

SAJ *makes a loop with the cheese wire.*

Put its little head through the middle and – pop.

SAJ *opens the box. The clucking gets louder.*

Give us a hand, would you, Rob.

ROB *takes one end of the cheese wire.*

CARA. Don't you dare.

ROB. It won't squirt blood on my shirt, will it?

CARA. Don't you dare!

CARA *rushes at them.* JAMES *and* KASIA *hold her back.*

That's my dad's chicken – my dad's!

SAJ. Then call your councillor, and tell her you withdraw your support.

CARA. But – but –

SAJ. Do it!

CARA *collapses.*

KASIA. Cara?

JAMES. Shit.

CHRIS. What did you do to her?

SAJ. Nothing!

CARA *goes into seizure.*

KASIA. Oh God, she's having a fit.

SAFF. Oh my God.

ROB. What's wrong with her?

SAJ. What does it mean?

HARRIET. Call an ambulance.

JAMES. Should we –

HARRIET. Don't touch her! Clear any furniture away so she doesn't bang her head.

KASIA. Oh my God.

SAFF. I feel sick.

KASIA. Is she dying?

HARRIET. It's probably hyponatremia.

ROB. You what?

HARRIET. Low sodium, you can get it from fasting.

SAJ. Will she die?

HARRIET. Not if we get her to hospital. Did someone call that ambulance?

Blue lights. The cast lift CARA *up and place her into a hospital bed.*

CHRIS, HARRIET *and* SAFF *stay by her bedside.*

A drip is placed in CARA's *arm, and a glass of fluid by her bed.*

KIRSTY *enters.* CARA *is groggy.*

KIRSTY. Oh my God, you stupid girl.

KIRSTY *hugs* CARA.

I was so worried.

CARA (*weakly*). I'm fine. It's fine.

CARA's *voice is weak and croaky.*

KIRSTY. You're not fine. Are you going to eat something now?

CARA. I feel sick.

HARRIET. That's a protein drip, it's a form of food. (*Of the glass*.) And sugar water. We'll get some solids in her when she feels better.

KIRSTY. Good. Here.

> KIRSTY *tries to make* CARA *drink some of the water.* CARA *turns her head away.*

> For God's sake.

CARA. How's Mum?

KIRSTY. She's on her way. But enough is enough. Alright? You've made your point.

CARA. But I still haven't had a response from Tesco.

HARRIET. You're never serious?

KIRSTY. Cara, Dad's memorial is tomorrow. At St Nick's. Remember?

CARA (*quietly*). I know.

KIRSTY. It's been twelve months. The family need you there. Are you really gonna kill yourself for Tesco? Do you think that's what Dad would've wanted? (*Suddenly angry*.) They already killed him.

> KIRSTY *stops herself. She wells up.* CARA *takes her hand.*

CARA. Hey. Hey, sis, I'm sorry.

> *Pause.* KIRSTY *composes herself.*

KIRSTY. It's fine. (*Pause. Wipes her eyes*.) We sold the farm.

CARA. Yeah?

KIRSTY. Yeah. We can go to uni. Both of us. It's over.

CARA. Right. (*Pause*.) What about the campaign?

KIRSTY. It's easier if you're alive.

> CARA *nods. She drinks some of the sugar water* KIRSTY *is holding.*

> SAJ *enters, followed by* JAMES, KASIA *and* ROB.

CHRIS. Oh, what are they doing here?

SAFF. Stay away from her.

KIRSTY. Who's this?

KASIA. We're her friends.

SAJ. We made a card.

JAMES. Recycled of course.

ROB. And we brought fruit.

KASIA. Organic.

JAMES. Yeah and local – cost a blimmin fortune.

ROB. We was gonna nick some from Tescos but weren't sure if you'd appreciate that.

SAJ. We brought a dictionary.

ROB. Yeah, get your five a day.

KASIA. Exams coming up.

JAMES. And Saj brought eggs.

HARRIET. Eggs?

SAJ. Yeah, laid by Jessie J.[8]

CARA. Who?

ROB. Your dad's chicken. That's her name now.

KASIA. We thought she looked like Jessie J.

JAMES. After she cut all her hair off obviously.[9]

SAJ. Though if you got her a little wig –

CHRIS. She's still alive then?

SAJ. Yeah. I've become quite attached to her, to be honest. Cute little things, aren't they?

KASIA. Saj has asked his dad if they can go free-range.

SAJ. Yeah alright, he hasn't said yes.

JAMES. But he's thinking about it.

---

8. If this reference dates the play it can be updated to a contemporary pop star – so long as s/he bears a passing resemblance to a chicken.
9. If the Jessie J reference is changed, this and the next line can be cut.

SAJ. I mean, we'll still kill and eat them, but at least they'll have had a nicer life.

CHRIS. Well, that's a start.

ROB. It's all you're getting, mate. If God didn't want us to eat chicken, He wouldn't have made it so delicious.

JAMES. Kasia thought she could make you an omelette.

KASIA. My own special recipe. Do you like chives?

CARA. I think so.

SAFF. What's chives?

KASIA. You're about to find out.

JAMES. Rob brought his camping stove.

ROB. I did.

ROB *takes out his camping gas stove and a frying pan.*

JAMES. I brought milk – fresh from the farm door, one hundred per cent profit to Mr Martins at Green Ridge Dairy.

KASIA. And I brought bread – baked by my mum. And she never bakes. It's probably horrible actually, but it's the thought that counts.

ROB. All washed down with a can of fizzy... mineral water!

ALL. Yay!

JAMES. So what do you reckon?

KIRSTY (*moved*). Your friends are lovely.

CARA. Yeah. Yeah, they're alright.

HARRIET. I'd better go and ask my mum. About the omelette. She's the ward sister here.

HARRIET *exits.*

SAJ. Cara... I've been meaning to ask... Did I... Was I... Did I make you get ill?

CARA. No.

SAJ. ...and have that... fit thing?

CARA. No, Saj. It was the fast. Low sodium, too much water. The nurse explained. You weren't to blame.

SAJ. Right. Good. Thanks. Cos I was feeling bad about that.

CARA. Thanks for looking after my chicken.

SAJ. You can have it back if you want.

CARA. Why don't you keep it?

SAJ. Really?

CARA. Yeah. The one that got away.

CHRIS. Just don't eat it.

SAJ. Eat Jessie J? Never.

HARRIET comes back with a tray.

HARRIET. Mum says it's fine. Just cook it on this to catch any mess.

HARRIET hands them the tray.

KASIA, JAMES, ROB and SAJ set up the gas stove on it and cook an omelette.

You sure you're ready to eat?

CARA. I'll have a little bit.

SAFF. Well, I'm bloody starving, I'll have yours.

CHRIS. I'm vegan, I can't eat eggs.

SAFF. Have some milk then.

CHRIS. It's all dairy, Saff.

SAFF. Yeah, I have never understood that.

CHRIS. I'll explain it to you one day.

KASIA. Have a chive.

KASIA holds one out.

ROB. He could hide behind one.

They laugh. Someone plays some music on their phone, a Jessie J number. SAJ produces some bananas.

SAJ (*of the bananas*). I guess this is dessert then.

JAMES. Did you nick those?

SAJ. It's a hospital, it's full of fruit.

HARRIET. You know, I never did find out why we share sixty per cent of our DNA with a banana. It must be because, somehow, if you go back far enough, everything is connected to everything else.

SAJ. That's deep, man.

CHRIS. Yeah.

SAFF. Shit, that means we're connected to mushrooms and they're disgusting.

HARRIET. I love mushrooms.

SAFF. Bleurgh.

JAMES. And celery.

CHRIS. Yum.

JAMES. Yuck.

ROB. And garlic.

KASIA. And gherkins.

SAFF. And horses.

SAJ. Of course horses.

SAFF. And farriers.

CHRIS. Farriers are people anyway.

ROB. Hang on, does this mean vegan Chris is related to a kebab?

JAMES. You can't be related to a kebab.

SAFF. You can.

JAMES. You can't.

ROB. You can.

HARRIET. No you can't.

ROB. What about after you've eaten it?

ALL. Eurgh.

CHRIS. I don't wanna think about that.

HARRIET. Just cook the omelette, man.

SAFF. Is there enough to go round?

SAJ. Jessie J only laid three.

SAFF. Just three?

ROB. Yeah she 'Did It Like A Dude' though.*

ALL. Aaaaah very good.

JAMES. Yeah but what was the 'Price Tag'?*

SAFF/ALL. Back atcha!

CHRIS. I bet it was 'Wild'.*

SAFF/ALL. Boom!

SAJ. Hey 'Nobody's Perfect' though.*

ALL. Raaaa!

KASIA. Yeah, but 'Who's Laughing Now?'*

ROB/ALL. Smashed it!

SAJ. Just shut up and cook, man.

The cast mime chatting while they cook.

CARA. And as the oil fizzes, and the eggs crackle and pop, a
rich, warm smell rises up – and I'm suddenly aware of an
unfamiliar feeling in my tummy. My appetite. My appetite is
back.

I open my dictionary. We're up to H.

Harvest.

Happiness.

Hope.

*As the Jessie J track fades up, and we leave them cooking
their omelette at* CARA's *bedside.*

---

* These lines are all references to Jessie J songs. If the play is being performed a long
time after 2014, and the Jessie J reference updated, this section can be cut, to go
straight to Cara's final speech.

THE DOMINO EFFECT

Author's Note

The play is written in an ensemble style, with a chorus of Narrators who can number anything from two to ten. Lines in the narrative passages can be distributed among the company as they see fit. Individual named parts can be doubled by Narrators, or can be played by separate actors. Smaller bit parts can be played by anyone, and the really small cameos could even be played by puppets, projections or otherwise suggested impressionistically. Cast size is therefore highly variable – though I would suggest a minimum of about eight to play all the parts and pull off all the effects required.

The play is written to incorporate dance and physical-theatre sequences. These can be performed by the Narrators/actors, or by a separate team of dancers. The intention is to achieve a fluid playing style in which we can move quite quickly through time and space. Dance and movement is intended to be part of the story, the story should not stop for it to take place. Similarly, all of the passages of narration are intended to be accompanied by a physical enactment of the stories we are hearing. Just because movement is not specified in the stage directions does not mean nothing is happening on stage. Indeed, physical movement is essential to bring the denser passages of text alive. I am deliberately vague about the onstage activity in order to allow the company to deploy their own imaginations in how to bring the play to life. Bodies and movement can even be used to suggest locations at times. Detailed naturalistic sets are therefore not required, and there should not be lengthy pauses for scene changes. Projected imagery or even simple stop-motion animation may assist with this.

The Domino Effect was first performed by Mulberry Theatre Company at the 2014 Edinburgh Festival Fringe on 4 August 2014, with the following ensemble cast:

ONSTAGE   BACKSTAGE

Jamila Ahmed   Afsana Begum
Tamanna Ali   Almitra Simpson
Naphysa Awuah   Naima Chowdhury
Maria Jahan Begum   Bipasha Islam
Tanya Hossain   Kinza Javaid
Naeemah Islam
Shahena Miah
Nowshin Sweety

Director   Shona Davidson
Movement Director   Lynsey Roddam
Voice Coach   Sarah Blumenau
Designer   Barbara Fuchs
Design Assistant   Rachel Roselle
Production Manager   Chris Stone
Company Manager   Afsana Begum

Characters
in order of appearance:

NARRATORS
FOX
MRS KHAN
STANLEY TROUT
PATIENCE ADEMOLA
JOYNUL UDDIN
MRS UDDIN
ALI MUSTAFA
MAHMUD NAZIM
JUDITH THE SHEEP
FAHIDA BEGUM
LAILA BEGUM
TOWER HAMLETS COUNCILLOR
AMINA RAHMAN
NABIJAH RAHMAN
SAMIT RAHMAN
MUSEUM GUARD
BOSS
DOCTOR
TEACHER
FLUSTOMER
THE DEBT COLLECTOR
POLICEMAN 1
POLICEMAN 2
ARTEMIS
LAWYER 1
LAWYER 2
ANIMALS
INTERVIEW PANEL
MUSEUM OF TIME CURATORS
GIRL/SURGEON

NARRATORS. On the first of March 1997
  At 7.03 a.m.
  A wild fox trots down Whitechapel Road, East London
  In the misty half-light of a Tower Hamlets dawn.

  Like a fox, these streets never sleep;
  Even at this hour they are quietly humming;
  Padded paws pass Jalebi Junction
  Firing its fryers to tempt early risers
  With caramel saffron, sticky and sweet.
  On past the butcher's, starting his bandsaw
  With the briefest of pauses at the scent of raw meat.
  Then quietly on past Cashino Gaming
  Mocking the dark with its bright neon wares
  Silently slinking past Crystal Gifts
  The owner inside lying prostrate in prayer.
  At The Blind Beggar pub the landlord locks out his lock-ins
  And bedraggled old men find the dawn a surprise.
  On past a café too cool for a name
  Where hipster baristas rub sleep from their eyes.

  The fox
  Stops
  Sits up on its haunches
  Right outside the twenty-four-hour Budgens
  Where grumpy Mrs Khan mans the till
  Day and night
  A woman seemingly devoid of all human needs;
  No food
  No drink
  No sleep
  Not even the bathroom.
  Nothing except spy novels
  Her nose buried deep
  In a different adventure every night;
  Tales of international intrigue
  Casinos

Assassinations
And fur coats;
A magic circle to keep the night at bay.

Pause.

For a moment
Time stands still
On the thirteenth of March 1997
At 7.03 a.m.
And fifty-six seconds
Fifty-seven
Fifty-eight
Fifty-nine
Then:
Bam!
Grumpy Mrs Khan looks up from her book
And spies the fox.

MRS KHAN. Shoo!

NARRATORS. And with that
　　Startled
　　It darts across Whitechapel Road
　　In a dark flash of red.

　　This event causes Stanley Trout
　　A domestic-heating engineer from Poplar
　　To swerve his white van into the path of a Vauxhall Vectra
　　Driven by Patience Ademola
　　A newly qualified family-law solicitor
　　On her way to an early-morning meeting.

　　The vehicles miss each other
　　And neither driver is hurt
　　But the resulting road-rage incident
　　(For Patience is patient in name only)
　　Catches the attention of halal butcher Joynul Uddin
　　Who, momentarily distracted from his high-powered
　　　　butcher's bandsaw,
　　Accidentally chops off two of his own fingers.

　　Mr Uddin survives
　　But the fingers cannot be replaced

Resulting in him having to give up
For ever
His beloved piano
His lifelong passion
And the one source of peace and beauty
In his otherwise monotonous and mundane life.

The depression Mr Uddin subsequently suffers
Ultimately leads to the break-up of his marriage to Mrs Uddin
A nurse in the neonatal ward at Royal London Hospital
Leading her
At the age of forty-two
To embark on a string of disastrous affairs
With several wholly unsuitable men.

Mrs Uddin's ensuing suicide attempt
Is the final straw in a hospital department beset by staff
    shortages
And a major contributory factor to the preventable death
Of Stanley Trout's premature baby girl Clara
A loss which plunges the domestic-heating engineer Mr Trout
And his wife Tina
Into an endless winter of alcoholism and debt
From which they never truly recover.

Pause.

Grumpy Mrs Khan
And the fox
Suffered no consequences at all.

Tick
Tock
Tick
Tock.

Pause.

On the twenty-seventh of June 1997
At 4.03 a.m.
Ali Mustafa and Mahmud Nazim
Two teenage vandals
Break in to Spitalfields City Farm
Where a sheep called Judith has just given birth
To a trio of baby lambs.

As Mustafa and Nazim proceed to daub the sheep enclosure
With graffiti expressing their loyalty to local gang
The Brick Lane Massive
The resulting panic among the sleeping animals
Causes all three baby lambs
To suffer heart attacks and die.

When the farm opens to the public at 8.30 the next morning
The sight of the three dead baby lambs
Upsets five-year-old Fahida Begum so much
That she becomes inconsolable
And has to be taken home.

Her mother Laila
An engineer at Bow Gasworks
Is thinking about this the following Monday
Causing her to neglect to double-check
That an important safety valve is adequately sealed.

The force of the subsequent gas explosion is substantial
    enough
To flatten three rows of nearby terraced houses
And knock Laila Begum to the ground
Shattering her left arm
Like a glass rod dropped onto concrete.
The arm has to be amputated
And the rows of terraces bulldozed
But the sight of this rare patch of open space in the East
London landscape
Inspires a forward-thinking Tower Hamlets councillor
To suggest the site as one possible area
For a future London Olympic Games;
An event at which Ali Mustafa and Mahmud Nazim
(Our teenage vandals;
By now grown men with families)
Are able to make a considerable profit selling fake 2012
    merchandise
In and around the stadium.

Judith the sheep, meanwhile
Is assumed to be genetically substandard
Sold to a local mutton factory
And made into dog food.

Tick
Tock
Tick
Tock.

Pause.

On the nineteenth of September 1997
At 11.59 p.m. and fifty-nine seconds
Amina Rahman
This story's hero
Is watching all this unfold
From her vantage point high up inside a storm cloud
At that moment drenching her soon-to-be home of Tower
   Hamlets.

For at this precise moment in time
Amina is not yet born
But is instead a tiny spirit
Observing the world she will soon inhabit
Trying to decide which unborn fetus she will possess
And which set of parents she will make her own.

Two actors step forward and become AMINA's *parents.*

She settles on Samit Rahman
And his wife Nabijah
A couple of modest means
But with honest hearts
He, a watchmaker by trade
Quiet
Studious
Precise
(And never late)
She, the opposite
Gregarious
Ambitious
And hungry for life's riches.

They are an unlikely match,
But then
The odds of any of us having been born
Are astronomically terrifying;
Like thinking about infinity.

The NARRATORS *think about infinity for a moment.*

They shudder and move on.

A clock chimes twelve times for midnight.

Then
At the very stroke of midnight
On the fourteenth of December, 1997
Amina is reluctantly forced from her mother's womb
Induced by a doctor
Two weeks overdue;
Hers is a reluctant birth.

For Amina decided long ago that this world she will inherit
Is unconscionably vile
Full of dog fights
Drunkenness
Muggings
And misery.

Take 1997 – the year of Amina's birth:
Tony Blair is elected
Lady Diana is killed
Great Britain wins the Eurovision Song Contest
Oasis release their third album
Channel 5 is launched
And a new-style 50p coin is pointlessly introduced.

This is clearly a world without hope.

So before she is even born
Our hero
Amina
Decides to withdraw
Away from the external world
And instead to live a life looking inwards
To a world of softness
Imagination
And possibility.

SAMIT *and* NABIJAH *stand with a newborn baby* AMINA
in their arms.

NABIJAH. No crying.

SAMIT. No.

NABIJAH. She's quiet.

SAMIT. Yes.

NABIJAH. A thinker. Like her father.

Clocks tick.

NARRATORS. After her birth
  Amina returns from hospital
  To her new home
  A modest rented apartment
  In a dilapidated Victorian block
  A former East India Company warehouse
  Echoey
  Damp
  A crumbling temple to the former glories
  Of an Empire long since lost
  Now council-owned
  And filled with her father's clocks
  Tick
  Tock
  Tick
  Tock
  A daily
  Hourly
  Minutely
  Secondly reminder
  Of the pointlessness and fragility of life.

The ticking clocks become louder and louder.

Eventually, they all chime at once.

AMINA *wakes in her mother's arms and starts to cry.*

NABIJAH. I think perhaps the clocks are disturbing her, Sami.

SAMIT. She'll get used to them.

NARRATORS. Amina's father Samit likes:
  Polishing his pocket watch;
  An Egyptian antique
  Sterling silver
  Engraved with its year: 1898.

He loves reading about his hero, Al-Jazari
A twelfth-century inventor from Baghdad
Author of
The Book of Ingenious Mechanical Devices
Instructions on how to build:
Water clocks
Candle clocks
Castle clocks
Elephant clocks
And even
The world's very first robot.

But most of all
Samit Rahman loves
Reading the notes on the back of his bottle of cologne.

SAMIT *takes out a bottle of Ajmal Vision and reads the back of the bottle*.

'Ajmal Vision
A sparkling fragrance
For men who exude passionate dynamism
Vision is the spirit of the young, energetic male
Dominated by musk
Cedarwood
And a floral fresh heart.

Macho music swells.

Ajmal Vision ignites the spirit of the wearer
With a burning desire for triumph.
A perfect companion for men who want to conquer their
    tomorrow
For the future belongs only to a few men:
The men with Vision.'

A triumphant crescendo.

SAMIT *sprays some into the air and breathes in the scent.*

NABIJAH *enters.*

NABIJAH. What are you doing?

SAMIT. Nothing.

NABIJAH. Is dinner ready?

SAMIT. Two minutes.

NABIJAH. I've had a long day.

   NABIJAH *sniffs*.

   What is that smell?

SAMIT. What smell?

NABIJAH. Like a dirty florist's.

SAMIT. Nothing.

   SAMIT *hides the bottle*.

NARRATORS (*whisper*). He is never brave enough to actually
    wear any;
   (*Whisper.*) The future, perhaps, belongs to other men.
   Amina's mother Nabijah likes:
   Home-made mint and saffron tea.

NABIJAH. Gram for gram, saffron is worth more than gold.

NARRATORS. Afterwards, she likes to read the future
   In the leaves at the bottom of the cup.

   NABIJAH *looks into the bottom of a teacup. She gasps*.

   At the weekends, she loves visiting the British Museum;
   The solid-gold exhibits are her favourites –
   She likes to try to guess how much they cost.

   NABIJAH *examines an exhibit, reading from the label*.

NABIJAH. 'Solid-gold crown, first-century BC.' Beautiful.
   How much do you think, Amina? At least a million.

   NABIJAH *catches the attention of a* MUSEUM GUARD.

   Excuse me? How much is this one?

MUSEUM GUARD.The exhibits are not for sale, madam.

NARRATORS. But most of all
   Nabijah Rahman likes it
   When her boss gives her compliments.

BOSS. An excellent cup of tea, Nabjiah.

NABIJAH. Thank you, sir.

BOSS. Just how I like it.

NABIJAH. Will there be anything else?

BOSS. Yes, why not. I'll have a coffee.

NABIJAH. Coming right up!

NARRATORS. Her ambition shines out of her;
    If the flashing light of Canary Wharf tower is the mountain's
      peak
    Beaming out its prize:
    C
    E
    O
    Then Receptionist is base camp
    And each cup of tea or coffee
    A milestone in the steep road ahead.

Clocks tick as NABIJAH *comes home.*

SAMIT *is fixing one of them with a screwdriver.*

    Coming home reminds her
    Of how far she has to climb;
    Draughty windows
    A birdcage lift
    The smell of damp
    Floorboards soft with woodworm
    And a husband as quiet as a stopped clock.

NABIJAH. Any sales today?

SAMIT *shakes his head, not looking up from the clock he is repairing.*

Any customers?

SAMIT *nods.*

Did they buy anything?

SAMIT *shakes his head.*

Then that's a visitor.

Pause.

Sami, I cannot support us forever. Our debts are piling up, like sand. We have a child now.

A young AMINA *is playing in the corner.*

NARRATORS. Amina stays quiet.

NABIJAH. How was she today?

NARRATORS. Though she is more than capable of speech

NABIJAH. Did she speak?

NARRATORS. She has discovered her power…

NABIJAH. Sami?

NARRATORS.…Silence.

NABIJAH. Are you even listening to me?

AMINA *casts her hands like she is casting a spell.*

There is a thunderclap.

Silence on stage.

AMINA *looks blissful.*

NARRATORS (*whisper*). But like all powers (*Whisper.*) It has a dark side.

DOCTOR *enters and puts a stethoscope to* AMINA*'s chest and stares into her eyes with a torch.*

DOCTOR. There is nothing physically wrong with your daughter, Mrs Rahman.

NABIJAH. Alhamdullilah.[1]

DOCTOR. Mentally, on the other hand –

NABIJAH. Oh no.

DOCTOR. Everything is fine too.

NABIJAH. Oh good.

---

1. Arabic = Praise be to God

DOCTOR. She passes all our cognitive tests.

NABIJAH. That's a relief.

DOCTOR. With flying colours, in fact.

NABIJAH. Really?

DOCTOR. Amina is a clever girl.

NABIJAH. Thank you.

DOCTOR. Which only leads me to conclude that it is her own choice not to speak.

NABIJAH. Is that a problem?

DOCTOR. This level of non-verbalism is quite unusual.

NABIJAH. You should meet her father.

DOCTOR. In fact, it is usually the sign of some terrible trauma.

NABIJAH. What?

DOCTOR. How are things at home?

NABIJAH. No. I mean fine.

DOCTOR. Happy?

NABIJAH. Very.

DOCTOR. And how are things at school?

TEACHER *enters*.

TEACHER. You see, Mrs Rahman, in some subjects, like art – which Amina's very good at, I should add – silence is of course not a problem. But in others, like English, or languages, some interaction with others is required.

DOCTOR/TEACHER. I may have to make a referral.

NABIJAH. What? No –

DOCTOR. Yes, to a specialist.

TEACHER. To the school psychiatrist.

NABIJAH. You don't understand –

DOCTOR. To a counsellor.

TEACHER. To Children's Services.

DOCTOR. To the police.

TEACHER. To MI5.

DOCTOR. To Interpol.

TEACHER. To the FBI.

DOCTOR. The CIA.

TEACHER. To NASA.

DOCTOR. To the International Criminal Court of Hideous Weirdos.

TEACHER. Don't you understand what this means?

DOCTOR/TEACHER. DISASTER!!

There is a disaster dance; everyone swirling around NABIJAH *and* AMINA.[2]

Eventually, NABIJAH *interrupts it by shouting.*

NABIJAH. STOP! I will sort this out. I will. I'll withdraw her from school. I'll give up work. Teach her myself. At home. I will make – her – speak!

The dancers go.

NABIJAH *and* AMINA *are left alone.*

Clocks tick in the apartment at home.

NABIJAH *takes out some school books.*

NARRATORS. And so it was that Mrs Nabijah Rahman
Gave up a promising career
To try to save her daughter from silence.

NABIJAH *takes out a child's alphabet – magnetic numbers on a blackboard. She tries to make* AMINA *repeat the letters after her.*

NABIJAH. A. A. A. A.

---

2. Optional.

NARRATORS. The tragedy was always
    That there was nothing she could do.
    For her daughter's protest was not with her
    Or her family
    Or their house
    Or her school
    It was with the world.

    Amina just didn't think it was worth her while.

NABIJAH. Please, Amina. Please. Just speak. One word. Not
    even a word.
    One letter. A.

    NABIJAH *takes the magnetic letter 'A' and holds it out.*

    A. A!

SAMIT. Nabijah –

NABIJAH. Go and sell some clocks!

NARRATORS. This turn of events meant
    That Amina retreated
    Even further into fantasy.

    It was a world in which nothing was what it seemed
    Where her father was not just a salesman of clocks
    But of time itself
    Where flustered customers
    Flustomers
    Burst in to buy themselves an extra fifteen minutes.

    A FLUSTOMER *bursts into* SAMIT*'s clock workshop.*

FLUSTOMER. Quick! I'm late for work. What have you got?

SAMIT. Quarter of an hour?

FLUSTOMER. Perfect.

    The FLUSTOMER *pays.*

    You're a lifesaver.

SAMIT. We have a special offer on weekends. Buy one hour,
    get one free.

FLUSTOMER. No time!

    The FLUSTOMER *rushes out.*

SAMIT (*sighs*). But there is all the time in the world.

NARRATORS. It is a world where Joynul Uddin
    The halal butcher with the missing fingers
    Looks mournfully at his dust-covered piano
    Which is actually an evil, ivory-toothed monster
    Filled with the bitten-off fingers
    Of everyone who has ever been foolish enough to try to
        play it.

JOYNUL UDDIN. Don't even think about it. Vicious
    contraption.

NARRATORS. It is a world in which the drunk homeless tramp
    Stanley Trout
    Is actually a traveller through time
    From somewhere long ago
    Somewhere dirty
    Smelly
    And medieval
    His endless Lottery scratchcard purchases
    Are actually attempts to find the right coordinates
    Which will transport him back home.

    STANLEY TROUT *scratches a scratchcard he has bought*
    from MRS KHAN.

    MRS KHAN *watches him grumpily.*

STANLEY TROUT. Fifty… twenty-five… ten… Dammit!
    I wanna go back to the past!

MRS KHAN. Get out!

NARRATORS. It is a world where grumpy Mrs Khan
    Isn't just a shopkeeper
    But a secret government spy
    In touch with HQ
    James Bond-style
    And able to call in back-up at a moment's notice.

    MRS KHAN *speaks into her lapel.*

MRS KHAN. Budgens to HQ, Budgens to HQ. Air strike required on Whitechapel High Street. T minus five minutes and counting.

MRS KHAN *makes a hasty exit.*

NARRATORS. All in all
It is a world of softness
Imagination
And possibility
Where no one but Amina is in control.

NABIJAH *takes out a packed suitcase.*

But then
One day.

NABIJAH. I've had enough.

SAMIT. What?

NABIJAH. I'm leaving.

SAMIT. Oh.

NABIJAH. Yes, I've got a job.

SAMIT. That's good. Where?

NABIJAH. America.

SAMIT. Oh.

NABIJAH. Yes, you remember Steve Jobs?

SAMIT. Who?

NABIJAH. Head of Apple Computers.

SAMIT. Oh yes.

NABIJAH. Well he died.

SAMIT. Did he?

NABIJAH. And I've been asked to replace him.

SAMIT. As –

NABIJAH. Yes, as the Head of Apple Computers.

SAMIT. Oh. Congratulations.

NABIJAH. Thanks.

SAMIT. When do you start?

NABIJAH. Immediately. I'm flying first class to Sillycone Valley.

   NABIJAH *takes out a silly cone and puts it on her head.*

SAMIT. What's that?

NABIJAH. A silly cone. It's what they wear out there.

SAMIT. Oh right. When will you be back?

NABIJAH. The corporate world is very demanding.

SAMIT. Oh. I see.

NABIJAH. Goodbye, Samit.

SAMIT. Wait.

NABIJAH. What?

SAMIT. What about Amina?

NABIJAH. What about her? She's fifteen. She needs to take some responsibility. And so do you.

SAMIT. Can you send money?

NABIJAH. Stand on your own two feet!

   NABIJAH *goes, slamming the door behind her.*

SAMIT. But I am...

   The slam echoes around the flat.

...standing on my...

   SAMIT *becomes unsteady on his feet.*

....own two...

   The echoey door slam gets louder.

...feet.

SAMIT *falls backwards. The others catch him and carry him away.*

NARRATORS. And as her mother's exit echoed around the flat
Rattling windows
And knocking against walls
Slowly
And silently
The damp Victorian box they called home
Began to express its grief.

A slow dance: the flat grieves NABIJAH*'s loss.*

Creaking
In place of weeping
And plaster
In place of tears.

Big chunks of plaster fall from the apartment walls, leaving gaping holes.

But as their apartment mourned
It also gave up its secret.

Inside one of the holes appears a very old box of dominoes.

AMINA *picks them up and blows off the dust.*

She opens them and examines one.

SAMIT. What is it?

AMINA *holds them up.* SAMIT *frowns.*

Dominoes?

Suddenly, there is a loud knocking on the front door.

Quick – hide. It's the debt collector! Cover your eyes, he's made of sand!

SAMIT *and* AMINA *hide.*

The DEBT COLLECTOR *swirls in. He is made of sand.*

DEBT COLLECTOR. You cannot hide from me!
I can pour through windows
Letterboxes

Through the tiniest cracks in the wall!
Look how much you owe;
These holes, they need fixing
These stomachs, they need filling
This rent, it needs paying.
Look at the grains as they slip through your fingers
Money
Time
Life
Tick tock indeed
Without your wife they've doubled in speed
You are running out of them all
And when they are gone
I will be back to claim what is mine.
I accept payment in sand
Suffering
Or SOULS.

SAMIT *holds a hairdryer at arm's length.*

SAMIT. Get back – or I'll blow you away!

The DEBT COLLECTOR *knocks it out of* SAMIT*'s hands.*

DEBT COLLECTOR. Pathetic! Pay what you owe, Mr
Rahman.
Pay what you owe.

The DEBT COLLECTOR *whirls off.*

SAMIT. I need more time.
Amina, help me.
We must put all the clocks in the freezer.

AMINA (*and the* NARRATORS) *helps* SAMIT *put all the
clocks in the flat into a deep freeze.*

NARRATORS. Tick tock
Tick tock
Tick tock
Tick tock
Tick... tock
Tick... tock.

The ticking slows down as the clocks pile up in the freezer.

Tiiiiick
Toooooock
Eeeeeeeeeeeeeeee. (*i.e. A 'freezing' noise.*)

SAMIT. Good. Well done. And now... now, I must find a job.

NARRATORS. Five simple words
    But with them
    Samit Rahman bid farewell to a dream.

    SAMIT *puts his coat on.*

    But before Samit can leave the flat
    Eeee[3]
    Head held high
    Eeeeeee
    And nobly shuffle to the Jobcentre
    Eeeeeeeeeeeee
    Fate intervenes.

    SAMIT *looks back at the freezer laden with clocks. It is groaning with the weight of them all.*

SAMIT. No – no!

NARRATORS. Too late!
    The frozen weight of all that stopped time
    Is too much for their woodworm-riddled floorboards
    Bent double
    Like a brick on a twig
    And with an almighty crash.

    SFX: Crash!

    The fully laden freezer
    Plummets through the floor
    And down through the ceiling of the flat below
    In an explosion of splinters and springs!

    They peer down into the flat below. MRS KHAN *is trapped in the wreckage.*

SAMIT. Grumpy Mrs Khan!

MRS KHAN. Help!

---

3. i.e. The floorboards groaning under the weight of the fully laden freezer.

Blue lights flash.

Some PARAMEDICS *take* MRS KHAN *away on a stretcher.*

Some POLICEMEN[4] *appear.*

POLICEMAN ONE. Samit Rahman?

SAMIT. Yes.

POLICEMAN TWO. You're under arrest.

SAMIT. I can explain.

POLICEMAN ONE. Can you?

SAMIT. No.

POLICEMAN TWO. This way, sir.

SAMIT. Wait. Amina – take this.

SAMIT *gives* AMINA *his antique silver pocket watch.*

To keep you going. It's an antique.

POLICEMAN ONE. Come on, sunshine.

The POLICEMEN *take* SAMIT *away.*

AMINA *is left holding the silver pocket watch, and the set of dominoes.*

NARRATORS. And so it was
At the tender age of fifteen
Much as she anticipated it would
The world abandoned Amina Rahman
And left her
To fend
For herself.

The NARRATORS *hand* AMINA *a* Yellow Pages; *she flicks through it.*

The dancers arrange an antiques shop around her.

A sign goes up, it reads 'Artemis Antiques'.

---

4. Can be played by just one policeman, who speaks all the lines, if necessary.

AMINA *puts down the* Yellow Pages *and tentatively pushes open the door.*

It creaks. The antiques shop is dusty and filled with junk.

AMINA *hesitantly looks around.*

ARTEMIS *pops up from nowhere.*

She is a grand old dame.

She looks a bit like a fortune-teller.

ARTEMIS. Hello, my dear.
I know – you can't speak
Can't or won't – it's a subtle distinction
But we don't judge here
In any case
Your thoughts speak for you
Oh yes, deafening they are
Some of the loudest I've heard
And there you were thinking you were quiet
Me?
Wouldn't you like to know…
They call me Artemis
Keeper of the past
Shaper of the future
For whosoever owns the past
Controls the present
And can therefore predict the future
Now
How can I help?

AMINA *holds out the silver pocket watch.*

ARTEMIS *takes it.*

A fine exhibit
Egyptian, if I'm not mistaken
1898 – a wealthy merchant's, no doubt
How did you come by it?
Your father?
Goodness me, and you want to sell it?
No no no no no
That isn't what he meant at all

It has a function far more valuable than money
Because it has brought you here, of course
To Artemis Antiques
Where all possibilities intersect
Now
The true treasure you are holding beneath your arm.

AMINA *indicates the set of dominoes.*

Oh yes
Allow me to demonstrate
If I may?

AMINA *holds out the domino set.*

ARTEMIS *floats over to it and picks one out.*

She cups it in her hands like a dice.

The domino effect
You understand it as leading to catastrophe
And it can
But learn its secrets
And it can also lead to triumph;
For these are not just dominoes
They are ivory eggs[5]
What hatches from them
Is entirely in your hands.
Use them wisely…
Watch.

ARTEMIS *blows on the domino.*

It floats out of her hands.

It floats towards a hospital bed being assembled by the NARRATORS.

MRS KHAN *lies unconscious in the bed, head wrapped in bandages.*

Remember Mrs Khan?

AMINA *gasps.*

Ssh.

---

5. Ivory if the dominoes are white, of course. Black dominoes would be 'ebony eggs'.

A pile of spy novels stand at the side of MRS KHAN*'s bed.*

A life-support machine beeps next to her.

One of the spy novels floats up and catches the domino between its pages, closing on it like a set of jaws.

ARTEMIS *casts another, and the same happens.*

She casts a third.

(*To* AMINA.) Upon waking
Grumpy Mrs Khan will find these mysterious clues
Nestled among the pages
Of her favourite spy novels.

We see this happen as ARTEMIS *describes it.*

Taking it as a deliberate communication
From a secret source
She attempts to break the code
And read the message concealed within.

With one domino in her hand, MRS KHAN *flicks through the first spy novel, cross-referencing the pages and words with the numbers on the dominoes.*

MRS KHAN. 'Return'…

She picks up the second book and second domino.

…'to'…

She picks up the third book and third domino.

…'work'.

ARTEMIS. Then
She begins to cross-reference.

MRS KHAN *picks up the first domino and applies it to the second book.*

MRS KHAN. 'Await'…

MRS KHAN *picks up the second domino and applies it to the first book.*

….'further'…

MRS KHAN *picks up the third domino and applies it to the first book.*

'Instructions'.

MRS KHAN *climbs out of bed in a hurry, her head still bandaged.*

A NURSE (*one of the* NARRATORS) *tries to stop her.*

NURSE. Mrs Khan, please, your injuries –

MRS KHAN. No time for that!
My Government needs me.

ARTEMIS. News of this naturally reaches your father's prosecutors.

SAMIT *appears in a jail cell.*

Poor dear man
Languishing in jail
Awaiting trial.

Two LAWYERS *appears with clipboards.*

LAWYER ONE. Apparently the victim has made a full recovery, sir.

LAWYER TWO. In that case we must reduce the charges.

LAWYER ONE. Yes, sir.

LAWYER TWO. Delete bodily harm. Put criminal damage.

LAWYER ONE. Right you are, sir.

We return to ARTEMIS *and* AMINA.

ARTEMIS. Pray
Hope
Love
And it shall be so
Your turn.

ARTEMIS *hands* AMINA *a domino.*

AMINA *takes it and cups it as* ARTEMIS *did.*

Choose a target.

STANLEY TROUT *appears, homeless and dishevelled,*
slumped asleep in a shop doorway, a begging cap in front of
him contains a few coins.

Ah, very good.
Now close your eyes
And blow.

AMINA *does so and the domino flies out of her hands.*
It floats over to STANLEY *and lands in his begging cap.*

NARRATORS. Ssssssh
Awaking one morning
From a night's cold winter slumber
Local alcoholic and tramp Mr Stanley Trout
Fishes through the coins in his begging cap
As he does every morning
In the hope that providence may have intervened as he slept
And deposited a gift;
A fifty-pound note perhaps
A meaningful job offer
His ex-wife Tina
Or even the spirit of Clara, his beloved baby girl
Whose loss remains
The aching hole at the heart of his life;
And where this all began.
Today, there *is* something there
Though not what he expected
A lone pair of dominoes…

Although not a religious man
Stanley Trout takes their mysterious appearance in his cap
As some sort of sign
And so, gathering his small change
Instead of buying his usual daily scratchcard
And can of lager
Stanley opts instead for a Lottery ticket
A chance to use the domino numbers
And see if his luck might change.

STANLEY *fills in a Lottery ticket.*

He hands it to MRS KHAN *at her till, her head still*
bandaged.

STANLEY. What happened to your head?

MRS KHAN. Shut yer face.

The Lottery draw appears on a screen somewhere;
STANLEY *watches it intently, clutching his ticket.*

NARRATORS. Alas not a single one of Stanley's numbers
comes up.

Disgusted, STANLEY *screws his ticket up and throws it
away.*

But the need to find a TV shop showing the draw
Has taken Stanley away from his usual begging route
And he finds himself standing next door
To Spitalfields City Farm
Which is currently hiring workers.

A 'Staff Wanted' sign appears.

Venturing inside
The former domestic-heating engineer Stanley Trout
Is so bewitched by the baby animals
Lambs
Chicks
Piglets
Even a foal
And so horrified by their freezing cold barns
(A condition with which Stanley himself is all too familiar)
That he is moved to offer his services
And designs an ingenious heating system
For the network of stables and outhouses
Powered entirely by the methane
Produced by the animals themselves.

STANLEY *holds up a complicated diagram of how the
system works to an interview panel. Animals moo and fart.
The interview panel give* STANLEY *the thumbs-up.*

This first taste of meaningful employment in over ten years
Infuses Stanley's life
With a warm rush of newfound pride and purpose.
And while nothing can replace the loss of his baby girl
All those years ago

Something about being around baby animals
New life
Every day
Connects him to a greater cycle of life
Death
And meaning
Which, slowly but surely
Ignites a pilot light
In the frozen boiler of his soul
And with it
Stanley's heart begins to thaw.

He holds down the job
He gives up the bottle
Finds himself a little bedsit
Until one day
He is even brave enough
To pick up the phone.

STANLEY *dials a number.*

STANLEY. Tina? It's me. Stanley.

STANLEY *wipes away a tear.*

I was thinking we could maybe... try again.

We return to ARTEMIS *and* AMINA.

ARTEMIS. Beautiful. You're a natural, my girl. Who's next?

JOYNUL UDDIN *appears, in his butcher's overalls, cutting some meat.*

Aha. This one I have been waiting for. About time.

AMINA *blows on another domino and it flies towards* JOYNUL *and lands on his chopping board. He doesn't notice it at first.*

NARRATORS. Early one morning
Digitally challenged halal butcher Joynul Uddin
Is chopping chickens into quarters
(Dead ones obviously)
While thinking about his ex-wife.

JOYNUL *strikes at the chickens with his cleaver with some force.*

When all of a sudden his cleaver strikes an extra-hard chunk
    of bone
He cleaves at it with extra force
And again
And again
And again!
Before finally the obstruction breaks in two.

JOYNUL *examines the domino, now broken into two halves right down the line in the middle.*

On closer inspection it appears to be a domino
Now perfectly split down the middle;
The mysterious appearance of which inside a chicken
Gives him pause
And makes him wonder what his supplier has been feeding
    his birds.

A customer enters – LAILA BEGUM.

His first customer of the day
(One-armed Laila Begum;
Former Bow Gasworks engineer
Now retired since her tragic accident and amputation)
Catches Mr Uddin
Examining the domino pieces with a frown.

LAILA. Good morning, Joynul.

NARRATORS. On looking up
    He spies behind her
    His beloved piano
    Long since silent
    Since his own tragic accident all those years ago
    Its lid now closed and covered in decades of dust.

    Only today
    It isn't closed
    But inexplicably wide open
    Its gleaming ivory keys
    And ebony sharps and flats

As pearly white and as jet black
As the day he bought it.

JOYNUL. Laila…

LAILA. Yes?

JOYNUL. You play, don't you?

LAILA. I used to.

JOYNUL. Come.

JOYNUL *sits at the piano.*

LAILA *holds up her one arm.*

LAILA. But… I have the same problem you do.

JOYNUL *pulls out a second piano stool.*

JOYNUL. Then together, we have the solution.

LAILA *joins him at the piano.*

They each play with one hand, taking one half of the piano keys.

They play a mournful yet hopeful tune, something like Debussy's 'Clair de Lune'.

NARRATORS. And so
Lost in music together
The world stops
Customers listen
Passers-by pause
As the music floats down Whitechapel High Street
Past the coffee-house hipsters who stop mid-cappuccino
The publican pauses while opening up
The morning air suddenly bright and fierce
With memory and regret
Past Jalebi Junction
Where even the deep-fat fryers stop spitting
And wipe away a greasy tear
Floating on past Cashino Gaming
Where the soft notes blanket the air
And momentarily silence the machines as soundly as if

Their very power had been cut
Next door, the owner of Crystal Gifts
Stops dusting his shelves
And his chest swells
With a love of the world and everything in it
The notes float
All the way down to Royal London Hospital
And in through the window of the neonatal ward
Finally reaching the ears of Mrs Uddin
Joynul's ex-wife
Who recognises her ex-husband's playing
Immediately
And for a girlish moment considers rushing down to see him
Her heart full of the past
But as soon as the thought occurs
Dismisses it as silly and unrealistic
What's done is done
And so she chooses instead
To sit and quietly listen
As the playing which was once such a part of her life
Fills the world once more
And for the first time in many, many years
She is happy
For a few moments
Happy that her troubled ex-husband has
Somehow
Once again
Found peace.

The music stops.

JOYNUL. Thank you, Laila. Now... what did you come in for?

LAILA. I... I can't remember. But that will do.

They shake hands.

We return to ARTEMIS *and* AMINA.

ARTEMIS. Lovely.
You are getting the hang of this.
Now. How about doing yourself?

AMINA *frowns.*

But you must.
Save yourself, Amina, before it is too late.
Your father languishes in jail.
Your mother is goodness knows where.
Do something for yourself, as well as others.

AMINA *opens her mouth, almost as if to speak, but*
ARTEMIS *vanishes.*

The antiques shop vanishes with her.

AMINA *is left alone at home holding the box of remaining dominoes.*

Clocks tick.

She looks around her.

She spies her father's bottle of Ajmal Vision aftershave.

She picks it up.

She takes out a domino.

She sprays the domino with a squirt of Ajmal Vision.

She sniffs it.

She grimaces and coughs.

SAMIT *appears, in a prison visiting room.*

AMINA *goes and sits opposite him.*

SAMIT *looks miserable.*

AMINA *takes out the domino and places it on the table.*

SAMIT *looks at it.*

He picks it up.

He sniffs the air.

He sniffs the domino.

A LAWYER *comes over.*

LAWYER. Good news, Mr Rahman.
Seeing as your victim has made a full recovery, the court has decided merely to issue you with a fine.

SAMIT. But I haven't got any –

AMINA *snaps her fingers.*

She indicates the domino.

SAMIT *looks down at it, looks up at* AMINA, *then takes the domino and sniffs it again, long and deep this time.*

Of course. I will pay what I owe. Like a man.

LAWYER. Good. The fine comes to a grand total of one billion.

The LAWYER *scribbles on a slip of paper and hands it to* SAMIT.

SAMIT. What?

LAWYER. One billion.

SAMIT. One *billion*?

LAWYER. One billion.

SAMIT. One billion what?

LAWYER. Grains of sand of course. The only currency we accept here.

The DEBT COLLECTOR *appears. He is larger than before.*

DEBT COLLECTOR. Pay what you owe, Mr Rahman.
I will add it to my weight
And let it fuel
My
STRENGTH.

The DEBT COLLECTOR *roars.*

SAMIT *grabs* AMINA *and leaves.*

SAMIT. Amina, do you still have the watch? The pocket watch.

AMINA *takes it out.*

SAMIT *cradles it.*

He notices it has stopped.

When did it stop?

AMINA *shrugs*.

SAMIT *shakes it. He sighs*.

Let's hope it is still worth something. This should be in a museum. We have to sell it. It is all we have left.

The cast build the Museum of Time around them.

Some of them become the CURATORS.

The CURATORS *are gathered around in a huddle, looking concerned*.

They are poking and prodding at the Universal Clock.

Have you ever heard of Greenwich?

AMINA *shakes her head*.

A wonderful place
Just south of the river
Where time was invented
And where it continues to reside
Looked after by the finest minds
Keepers of the Seconds
Counters of the Hours
Gatherers of the Days
And Guardians of Tomorrow.

SAMIT *sees the* CURATORS *in their huddle*.

That must be them.

He hesitates. AMINA *indicates for him to approach*.

But... (*Whispers*.) I'm scared.

AMINA *frowns*.

(*Whispers*.) These people are my heroes.

AMINA *takes the domino out of his pocket and hands it to him*.

SAMIT *gives it a long, hard sniff*.

AMINA *pushes him forward*.

SAMIT *stumbles into the Museum of Time.*

Ahem.

The CURATORS *turn round.*

The CURATORS *all have clocks for faces.*

They move with jerky, staccato movements, like a second hand.

Although they don't use real words, each new speaker takes a new line, like the NARRATORS.

CURATORS. Tick tock.
Tock tick.
Tick tock.

SAMIT. Forgive me for intruding.
I am Samit Rahman
And this is my daughter Amina
We have something which we hope might interest you.

SAMIT *holds out the pocket watch.*

One of the CURATORS *takes it.*

The others gather round.

CURATORS. Tock
Tick
Tick
Tock.

SAMIT. I hope it might still be worth something.
My daughter and I have fallen on hard times
And sadly we must sell it.

The CURATORS *hand it back.*

CURATORS. Tick tock.

SAMIT. What?

CURATORS. Tick tock.

SAMIT. But –

CURATORS. Tick tock.

SAMIT. Please –

CURATORS. Tock tick.

The CURATORS *turn away.*

SAMIT. Oh. Alright then.

Crestfallen, SAMIT *turns to go.* AMINA *blocks his way.*

But, Amina, they have bigger problems.
The Universal Clock – it's broken
And no one knows how to fix it.

AMINA *indicates the domino again.*

SAMIT *sniffs it.*

He braces himself.

He turns back round and addresses the CURATORS.

Perhaps... perhaps I can help?

CURATORS. Tick.

SAMIT. What seems to be the trouble?

CURATORS. Tick.

SAMIT. I'm a watchmaker. A fixer. Time is what I do.

CURATORS. Tock?
  Tick?
  Tick?
  Tock?

SAMIT. I see. May I?

The CURATORS *part so that* SAMIT *can examine the Universal Clock.*

He pokes and prods at it a bit.

CURATORS. Tick?

SAMIT. This is man-made.

CURATORS. Tick.

SAMIT. In London.

CURATORS. Tick.

SAMIT. By you?

CURATORS. Tick.

SAMIT. Then what makes it universal?

CURATORS. Tock!
   Tock!
   TOCK!

   SAMIT *hesitates*.

SAMIT. Right. Um... Just a minute.

   SAMIT *sniffs his domino*.

   Macho music swells.

   There is a greater timepiece.

CURATORS. Tock!

SAMIT. Yes.

CURATORS. Tock!

SAMIT. Not at all. The answer... lies in nature.

   SAMIT *takes out a copy of* The Book of Ingenious
   Mechanical Devices *by Al-Jazari*.

CURATORS. Tockety tockety!
   Tick tick tick!

SAMIT. No. Al-Jazari, the author of this book, was a twelfth-
   century scholar from Baghdad, the finest mind, and the true
   inventor of time.

CURATORS. Tock!
   Tock!
   TOCK!

SAMIT. There are rhythms in the universe which never stop.
   The whistle of the wind
   The regularity of rain
   The waft and weft of water.

CURATORS. Tick?
   Tick.
   Tockety?
   Tick.

SAMIT. You must find these rhythms, and channel them
   If you want to kick-start time.
   The answer – is an Al-Jazari water clock.

There is a dance to build a water clock.[6]

When the water clock is finished, SAMIT *and the*
CURATORS gather around earnestly. Someone pours some
water into the top of it and the others watch with baited
breath.

The water makes its way through the clock, and the
mechanisms start to turn.

There is a ticking noise, and the sun begins to rise.

The CURATORS *cheer – and lift* SAMIT *onto their*
shoulders.

Macho music swells.

CURATORS. Tickety!
   Tickety!
   Tickety!
   Tickety!
   Tickety!
   Tickety!
   TOOOOOOOCK!

NARRATORS. And so it was
   That Samit Rahman
   Found the strength to conquer his tomorrow
   For the future belongs but to a few men
   The men with vision.

   SAMIT *proudly sprays some Ajmal Vision onto himself.*

   The DEBT COLLECTOR *appears. He roars.*

DEBT COLLECTOR. Raaaaaar!

   SAMIT *roars back, louder.*

---

6. If resources prevent this, the following line can be added: SAMIT. I can build you
one if you like. And then go straight to the NARRATORS' next lines.

SAMIT. RAAAAAAAAAAAR!!!

The DEBT COLLECTOR *collapses in a heap of wet sand.*

ARTEMIS *appears.*

ARTEMIS. A triumph!

AMINA *smiles.*

And a smile. Even better.

ARTEMIS *indicates the domino box* AMINA *is still holding.*

Just one domino remains.

AMINA *looks into the box.*

I think you know who it is for.

AMINA *looks sad.*

Find it in your heart to forgive… and she will return.

The sound of a plane taking off.

ARTEMIS *vanishes.*

AMINA *stands at a fence.*

NARRATORS. And so it was that Amina Rahman
Found herself stood at the perimeter fence
Of London City Airport
The point from which her mother
Must surely have departed for America.

As tears of rage and frustration
Well up like an angry sea
She clutches the final domino tight
Before drawing back her arm
And flinging it with all her might.

It clatters to a halt on the tarmac
Next to a storm drain
Baggage handlers' trucks plough up and down within inches
But no one notices
No one stops.

SFX: *Thunder, and rain.*

The airport-runway gutter fills
And little by little
The domino is inched towards the drain
Before finally flipping over
To be washed downwards
Down into the dank, dark mystery
Of London's septic underworld.

AMINA. Nooo!

The cast gasp. It is the first time AMINA *has spoken.*

NARRATORS. But what Amina doesn't see
    Is this:

The tiny domino clattering through the filth
Spinning like a dice through the grey felt of the Thames
Tugged by turning tide
A wanderer floating East
Out into the heaving clutches
Of the grey-green nothing
Of the North Sea.

Nor will Amina ever know
That here, the ocean's ebb and flow
Causes her lonely domino
To catch the eye of a large grey sturgeon
Who, mistaking the tile for its usual prey
Sucks it down, out of the grey
And into its pungent guts.

Nor will Amina ever know
About the fisherman's daughter
Barely eight years old
Who
A hundred metres above
Floating on the water
Plops in her line
And prays.

Her prayers are answered
Though not in the way she imagines
The ten-pound sturgeon fish she lands
Contains within its belly

A find intriguing enough to catch the attention of a local
   reporter
In the daughter's sleepy coastal town
Where nothing much of interest happens.

The GIRL *holds the cut-open fish and the domino.*

She poses with it for a press photo.

GIRL. A domino! Inside its tummy!

*She is handed a newspaper featuring the story, then a
cheque.*

NARRATOR. The modest fee the fisherman's daughter receives
   For the double-page spread about her unusual find
   Is wisely invested by her father
   And eventually grows into a nest egg
   Large enough
   To send the girl to medical school
   Her lifelong ambition
   Where
   Through hard work and dedication
   She turns out to excel at Caesarian section
   An echo perhaps of her early life
   Gutting fish...

   In any case
   The girl's skills save countless mothers and their babies
   In hospitals around the nation –
   Including, in ten years' time, just maybe
   A mother in labour whose complications
   Give her diligent midwife due cause for alarm
   And an expert is sent for, to keep her from harm
   The young mother's name?
   Amina Rahman.

   But Amina would never know any of this
   Of the mystery she caused
   Of the funds she unlocked
   Or her own life she saved
   Instead she turns, despairing
   To brave the rain
   The uncaring concrete
   And the long walk home.

ARTEMIS *appears*.

ARTEMIS. You spoke.

AMINA *stops*.

You shouted 'No'. I heard you. You spoke.

ARTEMIS *removes her wig: it is* NABIJAH.

NABIJAH. Amina, it's me
Nabijah
Your mum.

NABIJAH *goes to hug* AMINA. AMINA *takes a step back*.
NABIJAH *stops*.

Your voice. I heard it. It's beautiful. Say something again.
Anything. For me. For your mum.

Pause.

AMINA. You left.

Pause.

NABIJAH. I know.

AMINA. Why?

NABIJAH. I'm sorry.

AMINA. Why?

NABIJAH. Sometimes… the world is just too much.
You don't get that from your father.
You get it from me.

Pause.

I failed at my most important job
CEO of your life
Forgive me
Please.

AMINA *takes out the magnetic letter 'A' from earlier*.

She holds it out to NABIJAH.

AMINA. A.

NABIJAH *takes it.*

NABIJAH. A...
    It's a good start
    The rest are at home
    Let's go back
    Fill in the blanks
    Talk
    Get to know each other
    Begin again.

AMINA. Okay.

They hug, hesitantly at first, but becoming a full embrace.

They let go.

NABIJAH. I feel like I did when you were born.

   NABIJAH *takes* AMINA*'s hand. They turn to leave.*

NARRATORS. And so it was
    On the third of August 2014
    A mother and her daughter
    Walk arm in arm through the rain
    The drops of a Tower Hamlets summer storm
    Hiding their tears.

    These streets never sleep
    But tonight at least
    They are calm
    Washed clean
    Satisfied
    That there is one more who walks them
    Who understands the power
    Of the domino effect.

    Pray
    Hope
    Love
    And it shall be so.

The cast each hold out a domino to the audience.

Your turn.

The End.

Other Plays for Young People to Perform from Nick Hern Books

Original Plays

13
Mike Bartlett

100
Christopher Heimann,
Neil Monaghan, Diene Petterle

BLOOD AND ICE
Liz Lochhead

BOYS
Ella Hickson

BUNNY
Jack Thorne

BURYING YOUR BROTHER IN THE
    PAVEMENT
Jack Thorne

CHRISTMAS IS MILES AWAY
Chloë Moss

COCKROACH
Sam Holcroft

DISCO PIGS
Enda Walsh

EARTHQUAKES IN LONDON
Mike Bartlett

EIGHT
Ella Hickson

GIRLS LIKE THAT
Evan Placey

HOW TO DISAPPEAR COMPLETELY
    AND NEVER BE FOUND
Fin Kennedy

I CAUGHT CRABS IN WALBERSWICK
Joel Horwood

KINDERTRANSPORT
Diane Samuels

MOGADISHU
Vivienne Franzmann

MOTH
Declan Greene

THE MYSTAE
Nick Whitby

OVERSPILL
Ali Taylor

PRONOUN
Evan Placey

SAME
Deborah Bruce

THERE IS A WAR
Tom Basden

THE URBAN GIRL'S GUIDE TO
    CAMPING AND OTHER PLAYS
Fin Kennedy

THE WARDROBE
Sam Holcroft

Adaptations

ANIMAL FARM
Ian Wooldridge
Adapted from George Orwell

ARABIAN NIGHTS
Dominic Cooke

BEAUTY AND THE BEAST
Laurence Boswell

CORAM BOY
Helen Edmundson
Adapted from Jamila Gavin

DAVID COPPERFIELD
Alastair Cording
Adapted from Charles Dickens

GREAT EXPECTATIONS
Nick Ormerod and Declan Donnellan
Adapted from Charles Dickens

HIS DARK MATERIALS
Nicholas Wright
Adapted from Philip Pullman

THE JUNGLE BOOK
Stuart Paterson
Adapted from Rudyard Kipling

KENSUKE'S KINGDOM
Stuart Paterson
Adapted from Michael Morpurgo

KES
Lawrence Till
Adapted from Barry Hines

THE LOTTIE PROJECT
Vicky Ireland
Adapted from Jacqueline Wilson

MIDNIGHT
Vicky Ireland
Adapted from Jacqueline Wilson

NOUGHTS & CROSSES
Dominic Cooke
Adapted from Malorie Blackman

THE RAILWAY CHILDREN
Mike Kenny
Adapted from E. Nesbit

SWALLOWS AND AMAZONS
Helen Edmundson and Neil Hannon
Adapted from Arthur Ransome

TO SIR, WITH LOVE
Ayub Khan-Din
Adapted from E.R Braithwaite

TREASURE ISLAND
Stuart Paterson
Adapted from Robert Louis Stevenson

WENDY & PETER PAN
Ella Hickson
Adapted from J.M. Barrie

THE WOLVES OF WILLOUGHBY
    CHASE
Russ Tunney
Adapted from Joan Aiken

For more information on plays to perform visit
www.nickhernbooks.co.uk/plays-to-perform

www.nickhernbooks.co.uk

facebook.com/nickhernbooks

twitter.com/nickhernbooks